Eagle Days

Eagle Days

A Marine Legal/Infantry Officer in Vietnam

DON W. GRIFFIS

THE UNIVERSITY OF ALABAMA PRESS

Tuscaloosa

Copyright © 2007
The University of Alabama Press
Tuscaloosa, Alabama 35487-0380
All rights reserved
Manufactured in the United States of America

Typeface: Goudy

∞
The paper on which this book is printed meets the minimum requirements of American National Standard for Information Sciences-Permanence of Paper for Printed Library Materials, ANSI Z39.48-1984.

Library of Congress Cataloging-in-Publication Data

Griffis, Don W. (Donald Warner), 1942–
    Eagle days : a Marine legal/infantry officer in Vietnam / Don W. Griffis.
        p.   cm.
    Includes index.
    ISBN-13: 978-0-8173-1578-8 (cloth : alk. paper)
    ISBN-10: 0-8173-1578-0 (cloth : alk. paper) 1. Vietnam War, 1961–1975—Personal narratives, American. 2. Griffis, Don W. (Donald Warner), 1942-—Diaries. 3. Soldiers—United States—Diaries. 4. United States. Marine Corps—Lawyers—Diaries. I. Title.
    DS559.5.G745 2007
    959.704'3092—dc22
    [B]

2007004148

In memory of Captain William A. Griffis III, U.S.M.C.
November 22, 1939–January 24, 1970
Brother at Arms

Contents

Illustrations

Preface

As a twenty-five-year-old Marine lawyer, I arrived in Vietnam on 11 June 1968, where I was assigned to the legal office of Force Logistics Command (FLC). FLC was a major supply base northwest of Da Nang that supplied Marine units operating throughout I Corps. By June 1968, the major North Vietnamese Tet offensive of January and February had been repulsed, as well as the "Mini-Tet" offensive of May 1968, and although the local Vietcong guerillas, as well as the North Vietnamese, had suffered significant losses, so had the U.S. forces.[1] Despite their losses, the North Vietnamese continued to pour men and supplies into South Vietnam in preparation for an expected large third offensive that summer, whose primary goal was the capture or destruction of Da Nang in order to create a more favorable position for the Communists at the Paris peace talks.[2]

While going through The Basic School at Quantico, Virginia, I applied to be an infantry officer as well as a legal officer. When I arrived at FLC, I became impatient to be in the field, and I soon had the opportunity to serve in the Provisional Rifle Company, which provided protection for the base. Fortunately, the staff judge advocate, Lieutenant Colonel Fred Haden, gave me approval to serve as the commanding officer of the company so long as

1. Jack Schulimson, Leonard A. Blasiol, Charles R. Smith, and David A. Dawson, *U.S. Marines in Vietnam: The Defining Year, 1968* (Washington, D.C.: U.S. Marine Corps Headquarters, History and Museums Division, 1997), 3.
2. Ibid., 1.

I also carried my share of the investigations, administrative discharges, and court-martials that were beginning to deluge the office. This was a great leap of faith on his part because FLC was the busiest legal office in Vietnam. In 1968 the number of cases tried each month went from thirty-two in January to sixty-seven in December. Of these, approximately one-half involved marijuana or hard drugs.[3] In this atmosphere racial incidents became more common, and "fragging" incidents tore at the fabric of discipline.

In Vietnam, I had the good fortune to have the best of all worlds. As a lawyer I had amazing freedom: I could climb on airplanes and helicopters as well as travel in jeeps and trucks throughout Northern I Corps to interview witnesses, and I could participate in court-martials. I learned how to be a trial lawyer in Vietnam, and for this I will always be grateful. I also had the unique privilege to serve with Marines in combat through the Provisional Rifle Company of FLC. In this position I was given wide discretion in planning and executing operations, and I had the opportunity to work with motivated Marines who believed that what they were doing made a difference.

A provisional rifle company was not the norm in Marine units; rather, it was created to meet a specific need. In the Marine Corps, the underlying assumption was that every man was first an infantryman. Consequently, all lawyers went through the same basic military skills and tactics training as an infantry officer. In Vietnam, however, there were not enough infantry units to meet all needs. Force Logistics Command was located within the First Marine Division's area of operations around Da Nang, but it had to provide for its own defense from close-in mortar attacks and ground probes. It did this by organizing the Provisional Rifle Company, which was composed of officers and men from FLC's various units who were organized so that they devoted part of their time to the rifle company and part to their normal tasks, such as driving a truck or clerking in the legal office. For ten days each month, one platoon would run day and night patrols and perform only infantry duties. During that same period, the men in the standby platoon worked their normal day tasks, such as working in supply, but at night they slept in ready tents, where they received infantry training and were on standby in case a

3. Gary D. Solis, *Marines and Military Law in Vietnam* (Washington, D.C.: U.S. Marine Corps Headquarters, History and Museums Division, 1989), 98.

need arose. The remainder of the company was available for call if necessary but otherwise performed only the normal duties of their military specialty.

As the commanding officer of the Provisional Rifle Company, I also worked with a small, full-time professional staff of infantry officers and men in the Combat Operations Center, which was located in a sand-bagged bunker. In it were the vital communications for the base, plus the command center that dealt with the perimeter defense and the patrols operating in the adjacent countryside. My position as company commander gave me access to a constant flow of intelligence about the types of enemy units in our area and what they were expected to do and when. Sometimes it was accurate.

When I arrived at FLC in June 1968, enemy mortar attacks were a frequent occurrence, along with long-range rocket attacks. Although the Provisional Rifle Company did not operate far enough from its perimeter to prevent all rocket attacks, it did, through a combination of aggressive patrolling, ambushes, and offensive operations, affect the enemy's ability to launch close-in attacks. From the end of August 1968 until I went home at the end of June 1969, prompt action by Marine patrols prevented the enemy from carrying out any further mortar attacks on FLC and interfered with the enemy's ability to attack adjacent Army and Navy units. These actions helped to keep the enemy at arm's length from FLC so that it could fulfill its supply missions to the Marine units operating in the field. The FLC Provisional Rifle Company was also a part of the perimeter defense of the Da Nang tactical area of responsibility, whose job was to keep enemy units from infiltrating and attacking important targets in Da Nang.

I began keeping a journal of my impressions and experiences when I arrived in Okinawa on my way to Vietnam. The dates in the journal either reflect the events of the day or give the dates that I found time to reflect on recent events. It provides the framework for these memoirs, as supplemented by after-action reports and citations awarded at the time.

When I came home I set my notebook aside and turned to the joys and tasks of practicing law and, eventually, marriage and raising a family. I basically put the period of my time in Vietnam into a back drawer until my longtime friend Jim Brown wrote his memoirs about his service as a Marine artillery officer in the demilitarized zone during 1967 and 1968. Jim not only urged me to begin the process of reviewing my own notes but also volunteered uncounted hours in reviewing this manuscript, both from the perspectives of a Marine officer who fought in Vietnam and as an author who published his own account of those events. Without his encouragement and suggestions, this story would not have been written.

Due to requirements of confidentiality, the names of the clients I represented in Vietnam have been changed. The events in which they were involved are faithfully recorded, however.

More people than I can name helped make these memoirs a reality. I owe Kay Holland a debt of gratitude. She spent long hours reviewing this manuscript and commenting on my grammar. As her pupil, I barely received a passing grade. My father-in-law, Dr. Ralph Chase, shared his valuable insight and support. Donna Russell, my friend and secretary, likewise worked late during the workweek and on weekends typing and retyping drafts. Without her help, this would be an oral history. Kathy Swain, as copy editor, toiled to make sense of Marine Corps jargon. Her efforts have resulted in a sharper, less-cluttered manuscript. Finally, I want to thank Dan Ross and the University of Alabama Press for believing that my experiences deserved to be published and for supporting me in this process.

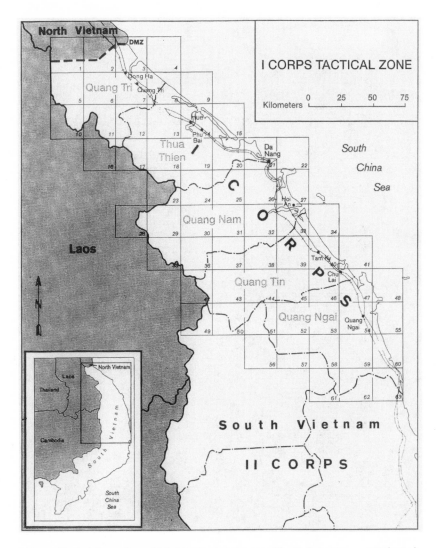

I Corps Tactical Zone. From *U.S. Marines in Vietnam: The Defining Year, 1968*, by Jack Schulimson, Leonard A. Blasiol, Charles R. Smith, and David A. Dawson. Reprinted with permission from the History and Museums Division, Headquarters, U.S. Marine Corps, Washington, D.C.

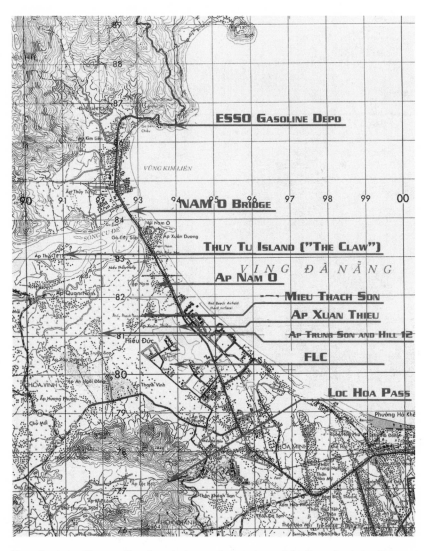

Force Logistics Command and tactical area of operations of the Force Logistics Command Provisional Rifle Company. Prepared and published by the Defense Mapping Agency, Washington, D.C. Reprinted by permission.

Eagle Days

1 / The Road to Vietnam

My journey to Vietnam began on a cold, blustery winter day in Sewanee, Tennessee, in 1961. I was a freshman at the University of the South, an isolated liberal arts bastion of learning in the Cumberland Mountains. It had just turned 3:00 PM, and I needed a break. Leaving the library, I strolled over to the student post office to check my mail and kill some time. As I entered the post office area of the student union, I noticed a Marine Corps captain and a gunnery sergeant standing by a table, resplendent in their dress blues. The mail was not up yet, so I decided to see what the Marines were doing. Other students were looking at brochures lying out on the table, and I pushed in and asked the sergeant what was happening. He looked me over with a skeptical eye and said that they were there to explain the many opportunities in the platoon leaders program but that it was open only to a select few. He suggested that I fill out an application just to find out about the entry requirements. Why not, I thought, the mail was still being sorted. Taking the application, I filled it out, along with a medical information form. Checking "no" to all the possible maladies, except asthma, I handed the papers back to a now beaming sergeant. The captain suddenly took an interest and began chatting with me while the sergeant reviewed the application.

Soon the sergeant returned with a concerned look. "Hey, kid, come here!" Motioning me over to the health application, he asked, "Do you have asthma now?" I told him that I did not. "Then go ahead and erase that checkmark and just say 'no.' It makes it easier to process the paperwork!" I quickly complied and soon found out that with the help of my new friends, I had just enlisted in the Marine Platoon Leaders Class (PLC) officer training program.

Sewanee football played a large role in leading me to the Marine recruiters; both were challenges. Although today a small NCAA Division 3 college, the University of the South (Sewanee) had a proud tradition in football that went back to 1899 when, on a road trip by train, it played five games in six days, beating the University of Texas, Texas A&M, Tulane, LSU, and Ole Miss. Later, the school was briefly in the Southeast Conference but had to drop out. With a student body of less than one thousand, it could not compete with the larger state universities. Nevertheless, in the decade beginning in 1958, Coach Shirley Majors led Sewanee through two undefeated seasons, and his teams were again a dominant factor in small college football.

At 160 pounds, I was small, even for Sewanee. Due to some need to prove myself, I decided to go out for the team, and I reported in early in my freshman year for preseason two-a-day practice. There I was introduced to practicing in the heat and humidity of late August and early September and the concept that water was for sissies. Coach Majors was a tough, no-nonsense coach and demanded perfection. Freshmen were expendable, and players like me primarily ran the opposing team's plays to prepare the varsity for the next week's game.

It was during one of these practices that I met Jody Gee. He was one of the team co-captains, a senior, and a little All-American tackle. Jody Gee was the meanest, hardest-hitting player whom I had ever met. He was well over two hundred pounds of solid muscle, and his forearms reminded me of Popeye's. In blocking practice I was put across from him. Jody Gee was so mean that he looked like to me that he always had a bad case of indigestion. I saw him smile only once. When he uncoiled with his elbow and forearm to my face, he snapped the bar on my helmet that was used for face protection, and all I saw was blood (mine). My nose was rearranged.

The following day I took the precaution of going into the locker room early to see the team trainer, John Kennerly. John was concerned about my red, bulbous nose and placed a clear plastic faceguard on my helmet to protect me from further direct contact. Feeling better, I trotted out to the practice field, where Coach Majors caught sight of me. "John, what is that player doing with that contraption on his helmet? Take it off!" In no time, I had no face mask, no protection, and, once again, I was staring up at Jody Gee.

This was when I saw him smile. It is probably not accurate to say that Jody proceeded to break my nose a second time, because it was still broken from the day before. He just added insult to injury. But I did not quit.

For four years I went out and practiced in the heat, the cold, the rain, and the fog. I did not realize it at the time, but the self-discipline that was being instilled on the playing fields of Sewanee was preparing me for other contests in faraway lands.

My Sewanee experience was important for other reasons that led me into the Marine Corps. In the small classes at Sewanee, energetic give-and-take was encouraged between the professors and students. Values were distilled from scholars who commanded respect. I thrived in this atmosphere and was convinced that the American experience could lead the world into the broad, sunlit uplands. John F. Kennedy was our youthful president, and when he told us that we should ask not what our country should do for us, but ask what we could for our country, I listened.

Ultimately, familial influence played a significant role in my enlisting in the Marines. My dad had served as a Navy armed guard officer on merchant marine shipping in the Pacific in World War II. All my uncles went off to serve as well. It was simply understood as I grew up that service to the country was honorable and that totalitarianism was evil.

My dad was the dominant light in our family, and my mother was the shining moon that revolved around him. Dad was a brilliant lawyer with a fine, inquisitive mind. Monday was the best day of the week because the Sunday *New York Times* arrived and there were lively discussions about current national and world events.

In this environment, books and reading were important. My older brother, Bill, and I were attracted to military histories. From an early age Bill knew that his goal was to attend a service academy and be a professional military officer. But there were no congressional appointments available Bill's senior year in high school, so he applied to and was accepted by the University of the South. Not until after his sophomore year was an appointment to the U.S. Naval Academy available. When Bill's friends were preparing to start their junior year in college, he was willing to start all over as a plebe. On graduation in 1964 he also was commissioned as a second lieutenant in the Marine Corps. Bill was meant to command, and the intensity of his dedication served as a bright example to me. Later, when he was preparing to re-

turn to Vietnam in 1969 for his second tour of duty while others were demonstrating, Bill referred to his upcoming tour as a great opportunity.

Then, of course, there was the draft. In the 1960s the nation utilized a
draft system to fill out its military manpower needs. Most healthy males over
the age of eighteen who were not attending college could expect to receive
a draft notice. As the gunnery sergeant pointed out that winter day, if you
were going to serve anyway, why not serve with the best?

The PLC program involved going to Quantico, Virginia, for two sum-
mers during college. If the candidate successfully completed the twelve weeks
of boot camp, then, on graduation from college, he was commissioned as a
second lieutenant. My early experiences quickly convinced me that the Marine Corps was a dysfunctional blend of terror and humor.

After flying from Dallas to Washington, D.C., for my first six weeks of
training, I entered the terminal in Washington and was met by square-jawed,
stone-faced sergeants directing the PLC candidates to a separate, roped-off
area. Signs in Marine Corps red and gold lettering indicated the quarantine
area where the candidates were gathered and separated from the rest of polite society. I noticed another boy from Fort Worth, Texas, who stood out
because, after reviewing the brochures on the PLC program, which included
beautiful pictures of the officers' golf course, he had decided to bring his golf
bag and clubs. I was not sure that we would have much free time, but I wished
him luck as we boarded buses for the ride to Quantico. Later in the summer,
while on a twelve-mile training hike in the steaming heat of the Virginia
forests, my platoon struggled along what was called the power line trail and
passed another platoon of sweating candidates going in the opposite direction. As the other platoon passed, I heard a clanking noise and recognized
the boy from Fort Worth. He had on his helmet and pack, and his rifle was
slung over his right shoulder. What was unusual were the golf bag and clubs
he carried over his left shoulder.

Ultimately, I graduated from college and was commissioned after complet-
ing my two summer training sessions. I was then deferred from active duty
while I attended law school at the University of Texas. It was during these
years that Vietnam was becoming a flash point in the world conflict between
Communism and democracy. As graduation from law school approached, instead of worrying about job interviews with prospective law firms, I prepared

for a different commitment. I would be assigned to Quantico for five months of intense training at The Basic School (TBS) and then would go into the Fleet Marine Force. After three long years in law school, the prospect of duty in the Marine Corps seemed very appealing.

I was assigned to Second Platoon, Charlie Company, at The Basic School under the command of Captain Jon Rider, a humorous and intelligent leader who would have been equally at home as a professor in a college class. We all wanted to do our best for him. He carefully brought us along and gradually prepared us for actual leadership of Marines in a war zone. During this compressed period of my life, two events stand out.

During the last part of our training our company held its formal banquet, which was referred to as "Mess Night." A major general from Headquarters Marine Corps was the guest speaker. It turned out to be a night to remember. All officers were in dress blues; red wine went well with the roast beef, followed by cigars. As we sat back to listen to the general, he said: "I am proud of each and every one of you. You are my young eagles. This coming year of 1968 will be the year of decision in Vietnam. This will be the year that we will break the back of the enemy."

Soon after graduation we received our orders and were assigned our Military Occupation Specialization (MOS) designations. I believed that I could be a lawyer for the rest of my life but that this was the time to be an infantry officer. The Marine Corps is primarily built around its infantry divisions, and those divisions were stretched thin in Vietnam. I applied for an MOS of 0301, which was the designation of the basic infantry officer, and applied for duty in Vietnam. Because it was a little unusual for a lawyer to request the infantry, the other lieutenants of Charlie Company were also interested to find out what my orders were. When the day came for our MOS designations and our next duty assignments to be announced, the entire company crowded into a classroom to hear the different orders announced, one by one. There were scattered cheers and catcalls as orders were read. When he finally reached my name, the company commander boomed out: "Griffis, D. W., 0301, Force Logistics Command, Fleet Marine Force, West Pac." My friends around me stood, clapped, and cheered—I was going to Vietnam. My wish to go to Vietnam was not only granted, but I received a double MOS as both an infantry officer and as a law officer. Prior to reporting to Vietnam, I was assigned to the twelve-week Naval Justice School in Newport, Rhode Island, and after thirty days' leave at home, I headed across the Pacific.

Making life even more interesting, the North Vietnamese and Viet Cong sprang their Tet offensive in January 1968, just as we graduated. It looked like it was going to be a long year. This is the story of that year.

2 / Going South

6 June 1968

My trip to Okinawa on my first leg of the prestigious, government-sponsored "Griffis Year Abroad" plan got off to a shaky start. There was already enough emotion in the air as I completed packing and loaded bags into the family car for the trip to the airport. As Dad clenched the steering wheel and Mom kept back the tears, the emotional level in the car soared even higher when I realized I had left my travel orders at home. Dad immediately wheeled the car around and violated all known traffic ordinances returning to our house and then back to the airport while muttering, "I just don't have any more cliff-hangers left in me!" With no time left for lengthy farewells, Dad's irritation melted into a bear hug while Mom and my little sister, Sallie, kissed me good-bye. I boarded the flight just as the passenger door was closing.

My flight across the United States took me through Dallas, Phoenix, and San Diego and to Los Angeles. As I checked in for the flight to Hawaii, I learned of the assassination of Robert Kennedy; he was shot in the Los Angeles airport shortly before my arrival. Throughout the airport, there was a sense of shocked outrage and bewilderment that this could occur. The flight to Hawaii was a reflective one. What happened to Camelot?

After a short delay in Hawaii, our plane, now loaded with troops, made its way across the ocean to Okinawa, which was the staging area for men and supplies going to Vietnam. On arrival, all the men were sorted out and assigned to temporary quarters until their scheduled flights to Vietnam. Everything that could be stored and left behind in Okinawa was inventoried and turned in. I could not help but wonder when and if I would see my belongings again.

After only one day in Okinawa, I noticed that the morale was off balance. Okinawa was filled with two classes of Marines: those going to Vietnam and those on their way home. Never should the two meet. The returning "salts" told their war stories to the warm bodies going out, waxing eloquent about the multitude of wounds, deaths, and other setbacks that could be anticipated. Naturally, these inspiring testimonials were meant to warp the minds of those who were more easily excited. Fortunately, those troops were processed through fairly quickly due to an ongoing major logistical effort.

I attended an officers' briefing the first morning. We were told that there were eleven North Vietnamese battalions in the Da Nang area, including sapper units with three months' extensive training. They were expected to attempt to get into Da Nang. We were told that the war from Da Nang north to the demilitarized zone (DMZ) was becoming more conventional as the North Vietnamese switched to larger unit actions in place of the small-unit, hit-and-run tactics of guerilla warfare.

7 June 1968

I have enjoyed seeing the familiar faces here of my friends from Quantico who are now artillery officers. We were able to share several evenings together and catch up on the news of those in our class who have already been wounded or killed. We discussed our assignments and what to expect. Last night, I visited at the "O" club (officers' club) with Ed Kliewer, Chip Brooks, Joe Fulgineti, Rich Foulkes, John Sabatier, Bill Lawlis, and John C. Martin. We watched *The Americanization of Emily* and then went outside to drink beer on the grass and to talk. Listening to them, I felt like a tourist in uniform because they were going to various artillery batteries throughout I Corps while I was going to a supply base, Force Logistics Command. Thus, I tried to talk everyone into a better mood. Ed gave me some film to send to his wife, and I told him that I would write her a short note. At 3:00 AM, I was awakened by a tremendous roar that sounded like jet aircraft were taking off from my cot. When the thunder faded in the distance, I knew that they were gone.

Okinawa surprises me. It is sixty-seven miles long and from two to fourteen miles wide. From the air, it appears to be dotted everywhere with buildings, roads, military installations, and housing. On landing, we taxied past brutish-looking, camouflaged B-52s, baking in the heat in their revetments, and a sleek Air Force jet painted a dull black that looked like the X-15 rocket plane. I imagine that it is being used for high-altitude reconnaissance.

Although trash and the odor of exposed sewage are a part of the ambiance of the teeming cities, the country itself is lush, and the scenery around the coastal drive is particularly beautiful. The water varies from light green to deep blue and is spotted with coral reefs and occasional fishing boats. At sunset, the clouds turn a fleecy pink and bluish gray, and the Pacific seems to live up to its tranquil name. The climate is humid, but constant sea breezes blow in. Even though the temperature is as hot as it is back in Texas, it feels cooler here with the breezes.

Next door to me is a Navy psychiatrist, Hugh Castell, who is going south on my flight. He is a Navy lieutenant and a good person. He has the honor of being only one of three psychiatrists in Vietnam with the Marines, only he does not exactly see it as such an honor. He is constantly trying to understand the Marines and thrives on war stories, but being away from his wife for a year and out in the boonies does not leave him tingling with excitement.

My roommate is K. R. Furr, a Marine captain who is returning to Vietnam for his second tour, only this time as an advisor to the Vietnamese. He is a reconnaissance Marine who was wounded three times on his first tour. K. R. Furr is a short, athletic fellow from North Carolina. Although he is mild mannered and has a quick laugh, I cannot help but notice a certain nervous hunter/hunted look in his eyes. He has been stationed on Okinawa before and took me into town last night to see the action.

We went to a steam bath first, where small Okinawa women stripped us and put us in a steam bath. After ten minutes or so, they brought us out, seated us in a chair, and poured warm water on us from a bathtub. We were acclimated to the water temperature. Then they lathered us down with a washcloth (their hands never touched me; I am not sure whose sensibilities were protected—mine or theirs), rinsed us off again, and put us in a hot bath to soak. Next, we were pulled out, put on a table, and massaged from the tops of our heads to the soles of our feet. The younger girls massaged our backs by walking on us. I felt like the village idiot as the masseuse walked on my ticklish back and reduced me to a giggling chunk of Jell-O. Then, of course, there are steam baths, and there are steam baths. Other places end by asking if the happy recipient would like the "special." Later we made a tour of the bars and strip shows, where the big attraction for the troops was American girls (round eyes). The captain did not drink and was fairly tired, so we returned at a decent hour.

8 June 1968

Another group of my friends from Quantico, the engineers and the supply people, showed up here on the way south. Rusty Hughes and Dean Marcellus, as well as big Jim Hartman, were in this group. Rusty is a true intellectual and a solid friend. He was one of my roommates at The Basic School. His dad was an ambassador. Hartman is a big, humorous, fresh-faced person from Indiana and is also going to Force Logistics Command. I enjoy his wit and look forward to being around him.

10 June 1968

Early this morning in the black of night during the middle of a driving rainstorm, I heard pounding on my door and immediately jumped up, fearing I had missed my flight. I noticed, however, that it was not 3:30 but only 2:30 AM. I stumbled to the door; it was Jim Hartman.

"Griff, you better hurry, they're already calling your name up at the 'O' club, and your bus is about to leave!" The time had been changed without notification to me.

Luckily, my gear was already packed, and I hurriedly dressed and shaved. Next door, Hugh Castell was less impressed with the rush and took his time with an air of splendid detachment. Captain Furr was also notified that his flight was about to leave, blowing his mind because he thought he was supposed to be leaving the next day.

Eventually, we all made our buses and wearily climbed in to make the long ride to the airport. It was still dark when we arrived, and after another predictable wait, we boarded a Continental jet just as the sun slowly rose in the east. In the background, B-52s lumbered off on their appointed rounds.

I slept most of the way in. We arrived in Da Nang about 8:30AM, where

Looking inland and west from Da Nang Bay; Route 1 is in the foreground; Force Logistics Command is on the sand flats around the settling pond, with a watchtower visible; mountains and Loc Hoa Pass in the background.

we landed on another big airstrip. The area was a sea of motion as sleek F-4Us glistened in their power climbs; transports landed and took off; and commercial airliners brought in one load or waited to take another load home. As we debarked, the stewardesses wished us a good tour and waved good-bye to us as we walked away past a transport loading medivacs from parked ambulance buses.

I hopped a ride on a truck to FLC, which was located northwest of Da Nang on sand flats, with mountains in the far background. After passing row after row of cramped civilian resettlement compounds, the city of Da Nang, cultivated plots, impassive civilians, and shyly waving children, I was introduced to my new home. Bunkers and barbed wire were everywhere along the way, as well as armed troops and military and civilian road traffic. As we crossed a bridge going to camp, we saw the remains of a French concrete pillbox, which had previously been destroyed in the French Indochina war, tilted at a crazy angle, reminding us of a long-ago conflict.

3 / Learning the Ropes

I reported to FLC headquarters at Camp Books and met the personnel officer. He looked over my record book and told me that he had been expecting me for several months. When I inquired about assignment to a military police company, he told me that I was assigned to the FLC legal office, which is part of Headquarters and Services Battalion. Lieutenant Colonel Fred M. Haden is in charge as the staff judge advocate, and his assistant is Major Mike Murray. The office is short of lawyers. There are seven lawyers, with four assigned to the trial or prosecution section and three lawyers assigned to the defense section. This FLC legal office tries all offenses that occur at Camp Books as well as the offenses that occur at Force Logistic Support Group (FLSG)-A at Phu Bai and FLSG-B at Dong Ha and Quang Tri. We are also responsible for trying cases arising at III Marine Amphibious Force (III MAF) headquarters, all of I Corps' Combined Action Group units, two U.S. Army detachments of the First Air Calvary Division located near Red Beach, and any cases arising from the Navy Seabee detachment, which is nearby at Red Beach.

After completion of the initial processing, I was directed to the Quonset hut that houses the FLC legal office. As soon as I arrived, I was greeted by friendly and familiar faces. Bob Wachsmuth was a classmate at the University of Texas Law School; Chuck Cherry and I had worked together for a short time at the battalion legal office in Quantico. The other lawyers were so glad to see a new face that I soon felt that we had known each other for a long time.

Jerry Cunningham and Chuck Cherry as they work on our bunker behind our hooch in late June 1968.

I moved into one of the hooches with Chuck Cherry and Jerry Cunningham, both of whom were from Tennessee. Now I had to decide whether to sleep in a bunker or the hooch. Our living quarters (hooch) consisted of raised wooden decks with screen sides and a tin roof.

The Viet Cong (VC) fire 122 mm rockets at the base and guide on two tall, lighted radio antennas that are anchored with guy wires. Our hooch lies between them and has a bunker located at the back door. The theory is that you wake up when the first rounds come in and sprint to the bunker before you are hit. One of my roommates was not quite fast enough two weeks ago and had to hurdle into a foxhole just as a round exploded on the other side. This round nearly obliterated the hut, and my steel wall locker, cabinet, and bed are now riddled with shrapnel holes. Nevertheless, I am going to be here for thirteen months and cannot let these minor intrusions psyche me out. My individual chances of getting hit are slim, and I think I will sleep inside the hut until common sense convinces me otherwise.

I am assigned primarily to the defense side of the office to represent Marines who get into trouble. Apparently the new and less-experienced lawyers go first into the defense section. When a defense lawyer becomes experienced or shows talent in handling court-martials, he is transferred to the prosecution side of the office. The odds favor the house.

11 June 1968

This morning I went out into poorly named "Happy Valley" beyond Da Nang to look at some Marine combined action camps and platoons. These involved small Marine units that work with local Vietnamese Popular Forces (PF), and they are generally run by young sergeants. The PF groups are home guards organized to help provide local hamlet security and are different from the regular South Vietnamese Army units operating in the field. The Marines add stiffening to the locals and help root out the Communist infrastructure. Since the Tet offensive, however, much of their work has been knocked out as the American strategy has begun to emphasize larger unit actions. We drove out to two different camps and a district headquarters. On the way we passed a PF training camp with mock-up helicopters and a confidence course set up to resemble the ones at Quantico.

Barbed wire, trenches, heavy-weapon emplacements, and individual watchtowers surround the camps. In the main compound, there is either a large tent or some type of permanent structure. Teenage-looking Marines without shirts man the dusty compounds, along with an assortment of PF troops, civilian dependents, and motley dogs. The platoons send out at least one daylight patrol and two night patrols and set ambushes every day. Their spirits are high, but the one camp that I visited was poorly prepared to handle a human wave attack from the Tenth Mongolian People's Horde. The barbed wire was too close to their trenches, and hand grenades could easily be lobbed directly into them. Moreover, the wire could be blasted through by a Bangalore torpedo and needed strengthening. There were no good clear fields of fire on two sides of the perimeter because huts were built right up to the edge of the wire. The VC could come to the perimeter without being detected, blow the wire, and be inside the camp. Worst of all, I saw M-16 rifles laying around outside rusting, as well as an M-79 grenade launcher, hand grenades, and ammo that had been strewn about indiscriminately that would corrode in the tropical humidity.

On the road back, we passed Marine patrols in single file on the paddy dikes and could hear rifle fire in the distance. Jets and helicopters flew over on their way to support operations at the other end of the valley some five miles away, but we were not allowed to go that far.

We passed a Buddhist funeral consisting of mourners, Buddhist priests, children, dogs, and two ornately carved biers carried on the shoulders of the relatives. This was in total contrast to the children running alongside, laughing and waving beside our vehicle, and to the stoic water buffalo peacefully plodding through the rice paddies. But then that is Vietnam.

Tragedy can strike quickly here. Tonight, while eating supper at the mess hall, I absentmindedly watched a helicopter whirl overhead, towing a cargo boom. The next thing I realized, it rolled over on its side and slid into the ground with a flash and billowing smoke. No one knows for sure what caused it to go down. There were no survivors.

12 June 1968

The war came closer yesterday. Last night the VC attacked Nam O Bridge to the north of us, trying to cut the highway. For hours we could see illumination rounds lighting up the skies with their stark glare, accompanied by tracers and the flash of artillery shots. Finally, the sky closed in, and rain fell in torrents. I could see only the faint glow of the flares through the storm, and the sounds became more muffled. This morning it appeared that the bridge was still intact while jets made dive-bomb runs on the surrounding hills and pounded the real or fancied positions of retreating Viet Cong.

Very early tomorrow I will catch a ride to the Da Nang airstrip and fly up to Dong Ha, which is south of the DMZ, to participate in an article 32 investigation, the military equivalent under the Uniform Code of Military Justice to a preliminary hearing to determine whether there is sufficient evidence to support charges being filed against a defendant. Dong Ha is a major Marine base and is in range of the North Vietnamese Army (NVA) artillery positioned north of the DMZ. If the field is under fire, I understand that the planes do not bother to stop but, rather, hit and roll while the pampered passengers sprint out the door, keeping a keen eye for a convenient hole. I hope my client appreciates to what lengths I am willing to go in order to stop the spread of crime.

14 June 1968

Dong Ha sucks! It reminds me of an oilfield camp on the dust-swept plains of West Texas, with a few added features. It is ten miles south of the DMZ

Outside the Force Logistics Command legal office after my first trip north to Dong Ha.

and the NVA and well within range of their artillery, so bunkers and narrow slit trenches are carved into the terrain everywhere. The earth is utterly bare of vegetation, and the constant traffic of tanks, vehicles, and construction equipment creates a permanent cloud of fine, red dust blowing over everything. There is no relief from the dry, furnace-hot wind blasting out of the north. The temperature is wilting, and one is soon thirsty, with dust choking the mouth and throat and coating the body. In addition, random incoming rounds hit the camp throughout the day, although no one pays much attention to them unless they get unusually close.

I departed from the C-130 transport and hitched a ride on a passing jeep to the legal shop of the FLSG-Bravo. The case under investigation involved an accidental discharge of a .45-caliber pistol by Lance Corporal Jim Kerr when Lance Corporal Allen Timms was posing for a "gungy" (warrior) picture to send home to his folks. Timms, the injured Marine, had two friends stand on either side of him with drawn pistols while he held his hands up. As the picture was snapped and his friends pulled the triggers on their "empty" weapons, Lance Corporal Kerr's .45 discharged and blew Timms's spine apart. He apparently stood for a moment and, with an amazed look on his face, made a half turn and said, "Oh my God, you've shot me!" then toppled backward. I will check on his condition today aboard the hospital ship *Repose* and see whether he will mend or be a paraplegic.

The tragedy is not only that of the victim but of the young Marines with their pistols. Marines love weapons and would rather have one in their hands than even booze and women. The pistols these men had were not authorized, almost certainly were stolen, and probably had been sold to them by other Marines rotating home. If the serious, and avoidable, injury to their friend were not enough, these men also face the possible criminal violations of un-authorized possession of firearms, negligent handling, and, if Timms dies, possible homicide. These young troopers are scared stiff, terribly sorry, and act as if they cannot believe this personal nightmare happened to either the victim or themselves.

I finished my investigation and warned the parties of their rights, handled four legal assistance cases, and caught a transport back to Da Nang. As we were boarding, an incoming shell hit the other end of the strip. In com-parison to Dong Ha, Da Nang now seems like a tourist destination.

15 June 1968

Last night I experienced my first rocket attack. It came at dusk, about 7:00 PM. The impacting rounds sounded like the pounding of a giant's fist on a door in an empty corridor. I was brushing my teeth and promptly ate the tooth-brush while running outside to see what had happened. At that moment, the ground trembled, and another explosion followed as a rocket landed somewhere off to my side and behind me; everything seemed to be happen-ing as if in a dream. I remember looking up and seeing the startled looks on two Marines who had just emerged from their hooch. I yelled, "Incom-ing!" and everyone scattered for a ditch or a bunker. Like a complete novice, I ran around, upright, looking for a hole to jump in, and I was decidedly not picky when I found one. As the noise died down, I rolled over into a bunker to wait things out. Normally (I am told), one can see the trails of the rock-ets as they come in, and they land in angry bunches; however, I did not see any trails behind these.

When we climbed out of our holes, billowing flames leapt in the sky from the motor transport area where a fuel park had been hit. The other rounds apparently did little damage, but, unfortunately, we had casualties. In the motor transport area, the rockets had knocked down an electrical wire, which was left hot on the ground. When a young driver jumped from his truck into a muddy ditch for cover, he was electrocuted. More personally, Lance Corporal G. E. Korson, one of our legal clerks, was killed, and several other Marines were wounded from a rocket explosion.

The scene was one of confusion for awhile as fire trucks sped to the fire, people shouted orders, patrols went out, and helicopters and artillery hit the area outside our perimeter. In the midst of this, I went over to the officers' club, where several of us drank the beer that others had left behind when they abruptly ran for cover.

After playing cards, I went to bed at 10:30 PM and slept fitfully until my hooch mate Jerry Cunningham shouted, "Incoming!" around 5:30 AM. I rolled out on my stomach this time, grabbing my helmet and flak jacket, and low crawled to the bunker. We took ten rocket hits this time, one of which was a direct hit on the S-4's office next to our legal shop. Thank goodness no one was hurt. I am becoming more alert to sudden noises.

17 June 1968

Everything is in better perspective now, following my baptism by the flying bombs. Saturday I tagged along with three of the lawyers who had work to do at Combined Action Group headquarters at China Beach in Da Nang Bay. I actually went swimming in the beautiful blue-green water. The beach is a good one, marred only by the barbed wire, bunkers, and low-flying helicopters. A group of young Marines were having a beach party, complete with footballs, Cokes, and piggyback rides for excited groups of laughing Vietnamese children, and their shouts and shrieks reminded me of beaches back at home. Out in the bay, junks rolled lazily in the swells, and it was very easy to forget the past night and this confusing war.

Sunday I went to church and thoroughly enjoyed the sermon. The preacher, a rugged man's man, was a Catholic chaplain who had served with the Ninth Marines in the DMZ. He read from the book of Job and compared Job's trials and tribulations with our present lives. He said that he personally had never doubted God's wisdom in making the laws of nature, the blue sky, or the green valleys, but he could never understand the reason for war, pain, and suffering. Still, he had gradually come to believe that God has given us misery and pain so that we can better appreciate the pleasant, beautiful things of the earth; we have fear and death so that we love all the more the vigor of life; and we have wars, in part, so that man marvels more at the blessedness of peace. God did not spare his own son from these trials, and our faith in Jesus will lead us through all our difficulties and to everlasting life.

Besides going to church, two big things happened to me Sunday. First, I was certified by the Navy/Marine judge advocate general's office in Washington, so I am now qualified to try general court-martials. Second, Major Murray, who is a big, reddish brown–haired Irishman and the image of the storybook Marine, took all the junior officers to the bar after evening chow. He kept us in laughter as he recounted some of the ridiculous excuses he had heard over the years from Marines who were in trouble. Most of the lawyers here are short-timers and are due to go home soon, but because I have just begun to enjoy this tropical paradise, I keep one ear alert for the sound of incoming.

The Da Nang coastal area is full of contrasts. Da Nang is sheer luxury compared to Dong Ha and other combat bases in "Leatherneck Square," the Marine bases along the DMZ, but it also shows the wear of war. The city, including the harbor, is ringed by a semicircle of land with sandy beaches and is topped by Monkey Mountain, where Marine communications and radar positions are located. Outside the city, the countryside is a network of hamlets and villages ringed by bamboo, set in rice paddies, and connected by narrow trails and a few paved roads. FLC is located in a sandy area, and this saves us from most of the red clay dust storms that are perpetually kicked up by wind and vehicle traffic farther north. Better still, the temperatures are up to fifteen degrees cooler here. When it is 120° in Dong Ha, it is likely to be a refreshing 105° in Da Nang.

Generally, our base, which is eight miles northwest of the city of Da Nang, reminds me of a large construction camp under frontier conditions. Scattered about are unpaved and black-topped roads that are either dusty or muddy, and on either side are the semipermanent buildings that serve as our offices and living hooches. The camp is ringed with barbed-wire barricades and pockmarked with bunkers, slit trenches, and fighting holes, and scattered around the camp are watchtowers and two tall radio towers, topped with red aircraft warning lights that the troops call the Viet Cong's aiming stakes. We

Taking a break during an operation on the ridges above Loc Hoa; Da Nang Bay, Da Nang, and Monkey Mountain are in the background.

are blessed with shower facilities, a mess that serves hot food, and an adjoining bar where cold beer and mixed drinks are available. Take away the rockets and the VC, and it is just like a barbed-wire Boy Scout camp.

19 June 1968

Last night I stayed up late and listened to "Hanoi Hanna" on a friend's shortwave, which was a real experience in lousy journalism. She is on the same wave band on shortwave that our Armed Forces Radio network has on AM. The news featured all the clichés: "Workers of the world united against U.S. imperialist aggressors and their puppets," "Afro-Asian solidarity," and so on. It was pretty dry, and its pseudo-intellectual level does not do anything emotionally to the average American. The program ended with a parade of victories past the listener, a report that described the glorious battles in the south of the "freedom-loving peoples" against the "American gangsters." With just enough truth in the reports to give them a shade of credibility, they are slanted and mention no losses at all to the Communists, so it is impossible to form any true picture of their reliability.

As usual, flares illuminated the skies around our perimeter last night as the VC probed us. Every night before going to sleep, everyone wonders whether we will get hit by a rocket attack and whether there will be enough time to sprint to a hole after the first incoming round doubles as an alarm clock. I now go to sleep relatively soundly and am only disturbed occasionally by the loud cracks of outgoing fire; nevertheless, some men face each night in their own private hells. One can walk outside and see the nervous glows of cigarettes in the dark as men gaze at the dark masses of distant mountains; they sleep in hot, mosquito-infested bunkers and wonder whether tonight will bring the big attack.

21 June 1968

Yesterday my schedule was packed from dawn to dusk with people to interview for coming cases, an article 32 investigation, and my first court-martial.

I defended a scared, nondescript-looking private first class who was charged with being found with a stick of marijuana on him. I called his buddies as witnesses and learned that all four of them went out to an off-limits village. They went to a house for beer and girls, but it was full, so a Vietnamese boy took them to another place. Here they had a beer, horse-traded (literally) over some girls, and then turned them down as too expensive. They had their pockets picked for their cigarettes, and when it became apparent that they were not paying customers, the girls called the MPs on them. As the story went, one of these Marines, not my client, apparently had as a girlfriend a Vietnamese prostitute who owed him money. These two were also in a state of feud because she was gracing another Marine with her favors. To remove the prior boyfriend as an obstacle while he earned some brig time, she called the MPs on these fellows when she determined the house in which they were transacting business. She bribed one of the children to plant a marijuana cigarette on her prior boyfriend, which in the dark was mistakenly put on my innocent. For some reason, despite my brilliant efforts, my boy was found guilty of possession of marijuana.

Possessing marijuana is a serious offense here because too many incidents occur when sentries go to sleep using it. Too many times Marines have been killed and their units attacked because of this dereliction. Thus, the higher command rightly looks with displeasure at this method of killing time.

Last night our FLC support group at Dong Ha had the hell kicked out of it by North Vietnamese artillery. All communications with them have been out since then, so it must have been a massive bombardment. Our own patrols around FLC in Da Nang are reporting frequent contacts on the sand flats and rice paddies, with blood trails indicating that bodies have been dragged away into the undergrowth. The night skies are often lit up like high noon by our flares.

There was a big fight near a First Marine Division's outpost that guards Nam O Bridge, which is north from our perimeter and which spans the Song Cu De River. Periodically Marines toss TNT into the river to detonate any underwater explosives or VC frogmen who might be trying to blow the bridge. This night, besides an explosion that damaged part of the bridge, they had a secondary explosion in which one Marine was killed, five others were wounded, and another went missing. Later we heard mortar and artillery fire and watched flares and tracers spewing out to break up an infantry probe on the bridge.

4 / Joining the Provisional Rifle Company and Early Legal Battles

22 June 1968

After eleven days here I am not satisfied with my passive role as a lawyer. Spending my tour here in the safety of a legal office is not the reason I came to Vietnam, and it troubles me that I am doing so little while others are sacrificing so much. I talked to the executive officer in charge of base security and applied to be the company commander of the Provisional Rifle Company. This group provides an outer defense line by operating both day and night infantry patrols in the villages and rice paddies outside our perimeter. I understand the company is looking for a successor to the present commanding officer (CO), and I want the job. My only concern is with Lieutenant Colonel Haden at the FLC legal office, who is primarily interested in seeing that backlogs of court-martials are handled. Nevertheless, I screwed up my courage and asked his permission to take on working with the Provisional Rifle Company as an additional duty to the responsibilities of my legal office. He thought for a minute and then said he understood how I felt. He had been an artillery officer in Korea before going to law school. As I suspected, his main concern was how much of my time it would take. Reluctantly, he agreed to let me assume the extra responsibilities on the condition that I would not let my work with the rifle company interfere with my duties as a judge advocate. He wanted to be reassured that I would not do something stupid and become a casualty. I told him that I would do my best not to let him down.

In the meantime, our patrols have been making sporadic contacts outside the base. The patrol that went out last night really fired off some ammunition. I will digress here a bit to say that the Marines on these patrols work in the different FLC shops and companies during the day as truck drivers, mechanics, clerks, and so on, but their real interest is to go outside our wire and take on the VC. These people are tremendously motivated and take pride in wearing their flak jackets and helmets and in carrying their "K-bar knives" while going out into Indian country (i.e., hostile territory) looking for action. One such happy warrior is Lucky Pierre, a court reporter in our office. Pierre is a highly enthusiastic, good-natured, sharp-looking young man who stomps off into the darkness every chance he gets and leads his squad, carrying an M-60 machine gun over his shoulder, John Wayne style. Last night on patrol they saw shadowy figures suspiciously moving in the deep black night. Pierre yelled out a challenge, and when there was no response, he cut loose with a devastating volume of machine-gun fire. The patrol knew they had hit pay dirt when they heard hoarse shouts of agony from out of the inky darkness, and later they found trails of blood. They never found any bodies, however.

This morning in the office a sheepish-looking private claims officer showed up, shuffling his feet and leading an indignant Vietnamese farmer who was demanding reparations because his prize bull had been chopped down while making love to a cow. The guilty party was a trigger-happy Marine on last night's patrol.

23 June 1968

My second Sunday in Vietnam, and I heard another excellent sermon, this time by the head chaplain of I Corps. The theme was morality and stressed the importance of keeping one's body a sacred temple by not giving in to lustful passion. This was a timely message to deliver to Marines in a war zone, especially for those about to go on R&R (rest and recuperation leave). Still, I am afraid this is one message that many put on hold until R&R is over.

We are building a newer and deeper bunker now behind our hut, which should protect us from all enemy rockets except a direct hit. It is also likely that any rocket will detonate first by hitting our modest home above ground before it actually hits our bunker.

24 June 1968

We are making good progress now with the bunker being built behind our hooch. We have hired four Chieu Hois (defectors from the VC) to dig, and already they have excavated a nice pit about six feet deep and eighteen feet long. We plan to sandbag and reinforce the walls; put in wooden beams, steel matting, and sandbags on the roof; and settle back for the fireworks. We hope our construction crew has not informed their former friends about our location.

Tonight the world seems to be slumbering in the heat of the Asian dusk, with only slight breezes whispering across the sands; there is a vague peacefulness in the darkening slopes of the surrounding mountains, which are outlined by a pinkish rose haze in the twilight. As I sit here sweating, the gathering gloom wraps its fingers around the silent vehicles and settles on the red glow of cigarette tips; I think of home, my family, and the rich expectations of the future. I also have an ever-increasing conviction that one must serve his country and fellow man, each in his own way, or run the risk of never having lived.

27 June 1968

Finally, I have had a change in my fortunes and have officially become the rifle company commander of the FLC Provisional Rifle Company. For months I said that I wanted an infantry unit and a chance to be more directly involved in the war, and now it has come true. I took my first patrol out today, and after viewing the people and their problems, I found that I do not want to shoot anyone or bring more misery into their lives.

My job as company commander requires considerable administrative work: drawing up four patrol overlays and plotting routes every night, signing reports, working a reorganization of the platoons, and getting a training program started. Also, I need to know the terrain, so I went out today on my first patrol to look the area over.

My assistant patrol leader was Sergeant John Montgomery, a young reconnaissance noncommissioned officer (NCO) who cannot wait to mix it up with the VC; I was also fortunate to have a South Vietnamese Army inter-

Rice paddy with paddy dikes that our troops tried to walk on.

preter, Sergeant Tran Min. We went out gate number 1, loaded and locked our weapons, and plodded through a seven-hour route that threaded through dense foliage. We went past strung-out villages with unpronounceable names, over paddy dikes, across sandbars, and by rice paddies under cultivation. The countryside is really amazingly beautiful. The paddies of cultivated rice are a refreshingly lush green, spoiled only by the reek of manure. One sees children and old people working in the paddies, with trouser legs rolled up. The normally distant hazy mountains take on a sharper and deeper focus. Invariably a little boy sits astride a water buffalo. The villages are a strung-out assortment of huts filled with old women and half-naked little children who hide and watch with wide eyes. Nowhere are there any young men, unless they have some kind of amputation. The young men are in the army fighting for either the South Vietnamese or the VC, or they are dead.

I am trying to instill a new spirit of professionalism in my men. They have plenty of enthusiasm, but they have not had enemy contact in a long time and have become sloppy and lazy in their techniques. They seem to think that, other than occasional rocket attacks, the war will not really hit here, but intelligence indicates otherwise. In the meantime, we will train and prepare.

Sergeant Min is a young man and big for a Vietnamese. He has a good

Young boy on water buffalo. Water buffalo were docile with children but could become aggressive if upset by passing Marines.

wit, is intelligent, and works hard. I detached him with a fire team to cross a wide rice paddy area and then to travel parallel to the rest of the patrol on another trail so that we could cover two villages at a time. What I looked for most in the villages were men of military age who could not explain their presence, whether the children and people were friendly, and the condition of the crops and their abundance. We note the families that have relatives serving with the South Vietnamese Army and ask questions about strangers in the area (you cannot be direct and ask if they have seen any VC, or you will only receive a negative reply). We also distribute C rations to the children, doctor cuts, treat minor diseases, and hope to win their confidence.

My interpreter met the patrol at the designated trail junction. They were leading a villager of indeterminable age (I always had difficulty figuring out ages) who had deserted from his South Vietnamese Army unit to return to his family. His wife and children soon came running across the rice fields to talk to the big strangers who were taking their man away. The man must have been in his late thirties and said he had served in the army for ten years and had left a year ago to come home to care for his family and build a house. I never knew if he told the truth, but I will never forget his look of silent dignity and how he carried himself in the midst of his burly captors.

He was thin, as most people here are, and had a nervous grin at first that later became a stoical mask. He was dressed in an old army shirt, sun helmet, and rubber sandals and sported a wispy Ho Chi Min goatee. His wife was highly agitated and pled repeatedly for his return, but I could not turn him loose after he had admitted being a deserter. The children came running, as if summoned by instinct, to see their father taken away, and gradually all twelve were crying and rolling on the ground. As I ordered the patrol to move out, a little boy tearfully came to me and offered five hundred piasters (about a $1.80) for his dad. All I could do was turn my back and walk off.

We also picked up another prisoner who was supposedly deaf and dumb, but his papers were signed by a hamlet chief who did not exist. It appeared to me that this Vietnamese could speak and listen as well as I could. We took him in.

What did we accomplish? We picked up information on the VC. In her grief, the wife tried to convince us how loyal the family was to the government as compared to others in the village. She told us of a woman who had two sons with the VC, information that we had not known, and also told us that thirty VC soldiers had come through the village only this past week and were in our area. She never would have volunteered this news freely; our patrol was a success.

30 June 1968

Last night in the command post while working on the patrol schedules for next month, we began to get frantic reports from the Army Air Cavalry maintenance and repair base to the south of us. They reported that their outposts had spotted thirty unknowns in the tree line to their front coming out of some abandoned houses and asked for our patrol to investigate. It so happened that we had earlier reports of enemy activity in this area. Accordingly, I had sent out a patrol to set up a night ambush in the area. We contacted them by radio and told them to move over to the suspected enemy activity to see whether they could locate any VC.

Before the patrol had a chance to move, we received another call from the Army. A hushed voice reported that the "unknowns" had split into three separate groups. Now we were even more suspicious and told them not to fire because we had a patrol in the area investigating their sightings.

A highly excited voice came over the radio and reported that the "unknowns" were on their knees and stealthily crawling toward their perimeter (even the Army support units are equipped with the latest equipment and had starlight scopes to watch the area after dark) and requested authority to open fire on them. This was the last straw. My battalion commanding officer grabbed the radio and told the patrol to pop a green flare directly over their position. He then contacted the Army base and told them what we were doing and asked them to observe the distance between our patrol and the reported enemy. Soon, a voice muttered back that the green flare was directly over the suspected enemy position and hastily rang off. The "unknowns" were my Marines, and they were very fortunate to have not been fired on by friendly forces. There were no enemies in the area that night.

4 July 1968

Independence Day! I have spent all of today in trial at the Fifth Communications Battalion, which is located at China Beach in Da Nang harbor. As we were coming back tonight in the jeep, all tired but relaxed and laughing over the events of the day, a strong surge of pride came over me. As we crossed the Da Nang Bridge, we watched red tracers, fired from ships in the harbor, arc high into the air and trail off into nothingness, followed by red, green, and blue clusters of exploding flares. This was like a vivid salute to a dream started some 192 years ago and caused me to think about the contrasts that were a part of this moment. We were once the revolutionaries seeking independence from a world power. Now, much like Great Britain 192 years ago, we are more like the elephant trying to stomp the mouse. With all our resources, we must provide an ideological alternative to that of the Communists. It takes a vision to change one, and unless we can instill the concept that democracy offers a better future, all our arms and money will be wasted, and the struggle will not be worth the effort.

5 July 1968

Yesterday was spent trying my first court-martial as prosecutor, which I won. We fought it out in a tin-roofed wooden hooch until early evening, with many sidebar comments, a surprise witness or two (which is forbidden in the military), and dramatic introductions of evidence. The case involved an eighteen-year-old, large and muscular, hang-loose Marine who, despite shortcomings, was personally likeable. He bought a stolen .45-caliber pistol and then went to a Vietnamese shop where he tried to exchange a broken shoulder holster that he had purchased a few days earlier. When the small, cute Vietnamese girl said she could not exchange goods bought more than three days earlier, he tried to grab another holster forcibly; when this did not work, he drew his pistol, chambered a round, and threatened to blow her brains out. Also, thrown in free with no extra cost, was an additional charge of assault and wrongful communication of a threat to a lance corporal.

As the prosecuting counsel I had to call an interpreter to question the girl. In the military, one first swears in the witness and then asks that person to identify the accused and point to him. But when I asked her if she recognized the defendant in the courtroom, she shocked me by saying "no." With sweat staining my uniform, I tried to rephrase my questions to get her to acknowledge the presence of the grinning defendant. After the fifth time, I had the interpreter ask her whether she could identify the accused; she brightly looked up, nodded her head "yes," and pointed to me. All this time, the defense counsel was vigorously objecting that my questions had been asked and answered negatively and that if I could ask my questions correctly I would not have this problem. I told the learned defense counsel that I appreciated the benefit of his sage advice and the fruit of his vast experience, but when I wanted his opinion on how to question a Vietnamese witness I would ask for it.

My problem was that it is considered vulgar taste by the Vietnamese to point at a person, and I had to work around the problem to finally get her to indicate her assailant.

There were many moments of thrill-packed surprises, but the one with the greatest flair occurred when the defense counsel took the three pistol magazines and, to refute the charge of assault with a dangerous weapon, tried to show that one of the magazines would not work as it lacked a spring to push the shells up into the chamber. He said that the court could not speculate on which magazine had been inserted into the pistol and that no proof meant no offense. Then, with a de Gaullist grand gesture, he tossed the defective magazine, which was allegedly missing its spring, onto the table in front of the court-martial panel. As he turned to stalk away, the magazine spring, which had been rusted to the bottom of the magazine, neatly popped out. Guilty!

One aspect of the legal proceedings here that stands out in my mind is the work of the court reporters. Instead of dictating into a handheld microphone, they talk into a face mask that covers their mouth and nose and do almost simultaneous repeats of every question and answer, which are recorded on a disk. It is disconcerting the first time one experiences it because it sounds like an echo of what is being said. It also has to be very wearing on the court reporters because the temperatures are often over 100° in the tent or hut where the proceedings occur, and they are almost choking in their own sweat in their masks before a hearing is finished.

7 July 1968

Out of nowhere I received a call from Jim Brown, my great friend from my college years at Sewanee. He knew that I was stationed at the FLC legal office in Da Nang and called me from the transit area at the Da Nang air base while waiting to catch a plane home. He then hitched a ride to FLC. Jim looked tired and had lost weight during his tour as an artillery forward observer and as the commanding officer of Charlie Battery in the DMZ. His battery was recently lifted by helicopters into a landing zone to provide close artillery support to a Marine infantry regiment operating close to the Laotian border. They ran into a definite problem when nightfall found them in an isolated position in the middle of enemy territory and without any Marine infantry support. The situation was so critical that the commanding general of the Third Marine Division, General Raymond Davis, flew in by helicopter to look over their position and to warn Jim personally that he had better get ready; before the operation was over, the NVA would attack in an attempt to overrun his position and capture his guns.

On the second night of their stay at the landing zone, which was named Torch, a large enemy unit attacked the Marines from two directions and tried to isolate Jim and his gunners into small groups that could then be overrun. The fighting was furious, and the enemy forced their way into the Marines' position. An NVA sapper tossed a satchel charge, which exploded and then stunned Jim. This was followed by the flash of a concussion grenade, which burned his face and eyes. Jim rallied his men, and they counterattacked. Jim told me that some of his men were so excited that he had to yell for them to shoot because they were forgetting to fire. When one Marine's M-16 rifle jammed, Jim told him to put a bayonet on it and get back into the fight. Despite his own wounds, Jim moved constantly from position to position, shouting orders and encouragement. The NVA were all around and penetrated to the gun positions, where six or seven of them were killed in hand-to-hand combat. At dawn, the NVA withdrew, leaving twenty-three in the barbed wire, six near the guns, and trails of blood leading away into the elephant grass. The Marines lost one-third of their force, but at dawn's light they were still standing after defeating a force many times their size. The North Vietnamese never took their guns. As a result Jim has earned a purple heart and has been recommended for a silver star.

For all the hell he has been through and with the constant strain and tension of the front and the closeness of death, Jim has not noticeably changed. He is a natural leader. He looked forward to going home and rejoining his wife and family, and we made small talk about plans for the future when we could get together again. We waved at each other as he drove off in the back of a truck, headed for the Da Nang airport and his flight home. Through the dust, I thanked God for bringing Jim safely through his days in the DMZ.

Our patrol found a booby trap last night alongside the trail. The point man rubbed his leg alongside the trip wire but did not detonate it. We have been receiving intelligence reports now for days concerning increased enemy activity in our area and a possible ground probe. Snipers have been harassing us regularly, but I hate like hell for booby traps to appear now. The price of admission to this great adventure is going up.

15 July 1968

It is difficult to believe that more than a week has passed since I last had the chance to write. I have been so busy I simply have not had the opportunity. Last Monday I caught a transport north to Dong Ha to run two article 32 investigations and, after spending the night there, returned the following day. It was not as windy or as noticeably dusty as my last trip, but within hours the sweat and dust had caked a surface of grime over everything on me. On the accidental discharge case of Lance Corporal Kerr, it looks as if he will be charged with assault with a deadly weapon and assault with intent to kill.

The victim is now paralyzed from the waist down and is in the naval hospital in Japan, where I suppose I will have the chance to go to interview him because he can not come here.

Wednesday night we had a surprise alert for my infantry company. I notified my platoon commanders, and they rapidly assembled their men in the vehicles for immediate reaction. It took us thirty minutes, but we can cut this time in half. Nevertheless, my CO said it was the best drill he had seen and apparently was pleased.

19 July 1968

The night before last, one of our patrols was walking on a rice paddy dike and found a VC asleep. He had three hand grenades on him and acted a bit confused about the whole situation. I am too. It is hard to believe that a person could go to sleep out in the open near a Marine base and let one of our patrols walk up on him without him waking up. He was carefully aroused and brought in for questioning.

Last night I appeared before an administrative discharge board to defend a nineteen-year-old young rebel from receiving an undesirable discharge. After it was over, around 9 PM, I walked into the mess hall, where I was informed that the command post was trying to reach me. I immediately called in, and the security officer informed me that the ready platoon had been called out to try to apprehend some VC seen moving onto an island near the reservoir at the edge of our base. The first report estimated that there was a force of thirty, but it was subsequently revised to five suspected VC. We have all been skittish because of a supposed enemy offensive in the offing, so I ran over to my hut, grabbed my gear, and sprinted to the command post bunker to get a fix on the situation. When I arrived, I saw that the ready platoon was already mounted in the trucks, and they were starting to roll; I had time only to grab a rifle and jump on the closest truck before we were off in a cloud of dust.

We sped down Highway 1 with our lights off until we reached a sandbar with a Buddhist graveyard. We debarked quietly, and when I saw I was the only officer present, I organized the men into their squads and started them moving into the area. None of us knew what to expect, so we locked and loaded. I had two squads with me at the time, with another on the highway in a blocking position. I tried to move one squad through the island while I positioned machine guns on the sand dunes overlooking the graveyard and had another squad ready to stop anyone who tried to flee.

This little episode showed me that confusion is a characteristic of war. All this time my radioman was receiving frantic calls from the base command post wanting to know our situation and position. I did not know our position, and the situation was obscure. They asked where I was from Thrust Point Alpha, but I had never been told where Alpha was. My radio operator did not know the call signs and had trouble with the radio; I had to take it over and operate it myself. We called in illumination rounds, and I adjusted the fire, but then the heavy metal canisters that hold the parachute flares began to land right in our position, slamming into the ground all around us. We had to stop the illumination and adjust to the dark. The squad that I sent to sweep the island went about fifty yards and discovered that the island was, in fact, a mangrove swamp and that they were chest deep in the mire. I pulled them back and sent them around to the other side of the island to try again. My battalion commanding officer, by now on the phone and alternatively half mad or half hysterical, wanted to know why I had not swept through the area. My squad went in on the other side of the swamp and again were submerged, so I pulled them back and placed them on one end of the sand dunes overlooking the swamp/island. The squad I was with continued to be broadside to the long axis of the island, and I called up the remaining squad to seal off the other end of the island. The only way the VC had to escape (if they were still there) would be to swim. I radioed back that we would cordon the area until dawn and then sweep through it.

Next, I trooped the lines, making sure the men were in the right positions, especially those who manned the machine guns and the M-79 grenade launchers. I had them set in twos and put them on 50 percent alert, with one sleeping and one awake. Then I went back and tried to catch some shut-eye myself. I had my radio operator wake me up every hour, at which time I went along the line checking the sets of men to be sure they were alert. It took thirty minutes to walk the lines each time, and as morning drew closer, I frequently found both men in the sets asleep in their holes. The sweat dried on me, and the night grew cool, leaving a chill in my bones. Several times we heard the birds on the island start squawking as if someone were moving, and we heard branches snapping. The night seemed to last forever, but finally the faint tint of dawn appeared. Suddenly, everyone became alert, and daylight came so fast it reminded me of Kipling's poem "Mandalay" with the verse "An' the dawn comes up like thunder outer China 'crost the Bay." With the chirping of the birds as a background and in the early morning haze rising from the green swamp, I sent two squads floundering through to one end of the island and then back through again. They returned completely soaked, their weapons clogged with mud; all they found were footprints. Whoever had been there had had plenty of chances to make their exits while we were on the way out, while we were trying to close the cordon, and when my men were fatigued in the predawn hours.

At the least, it is apparent now that we can react in a fairly short time to reported movements, and I know more about the surrounding terrain and the problems of moving men through it at night. I also feel for anyone else who has to spend his sleeping hours roaming the countryside looking for things that go bump in the night.

20 July 1968

Hurray! The dogsled via the North Pole finally came in with my promotion to captain! I just received a phone call from FLC headquarters that it had arrived with my date of rank backdated to 1 July 1967. Great news!

23 July 1968

On the twenty-first, I had my first general court-martial, managed to blunder through, and came out on top. It involved Lance Corporal Russell Smythe, a mousy-looking Marine who was caught in a scivy house (house of prostitution) in the village in violation of the curfew and off-limits regulations and without his weapon; however, the main thing the authorities jumped him for was possession of marijuana. My theory was that it had been planted on him when he was mistaken for another in the group whose jilted whore wanted to frame him for the "monkey-house" (the brig). The troopers who gave their testimony to the respectable assemblage of colonels and majors told it like it was. The Marines used every rank, raw adjective that troopers always use, describing in detail how they had violated every rule to go out into the village for "boom boom" or "leg" (referencing the female anatomy) and booze and giving a firsthand description of a boy's night on the town. The court was fascinated, and the members strained to hear every word. The best witness for me, and the man who won my case, was a young, skinny, awkward Marine who spoke a mile a minute when excited and had a sense of humor that could crack granite. The government's counsel made the mistake of asking that one last question when he asked Blythe (this witness) how he could know whether Smythe (the accused) would use pot, and in fact, how did the court know that Blythe did not use it himself? Blythe proceeded to tell the court that before joining the Marine Corps, he had worked for U.S., New York State, and New York City agencies in Harlem for the last three years trying to rehabilitate dope addicts. He stated that he worked with his godfather, a Catholic priest, and that Smythe came out to work with them for one summer as a drug counselor. Next case.

5 / The Chief of Staff Loses His Jeep

Shortly after becoming a trial/defense counsel at FLC, I was handed a hot potato in the form of a young corporal accused of stealing the chief of staff's jeep. Although the MPs caught the suspect off base after curfew and in an off-limits area, this was a case that appealed to me. It looked to me like a rush job by higher-ups to hang the corporal as an example.

When I met Corporal Mike Slaughter, I found him to be clean cut, decent, intelligent, and a pleasure to work with. He was an Eagle Scout. Although General Harry Olson, the commanding officer at FLC, appeared to be upset that his chief's jeep was found parked outside a skivy house and tended to believe that the command driver (Corporal Slaughter) was the culprit, I believed Slaughter. In fact, I felt good about defending the corporal instead of the typical "pot" hound. Slaughter's sincerity, his prior clean record, and his appearance all led me to believe that the command was trying to push through a plea bargain that would be a huge injustice.

In the process of seeking justice, I talked to Colonel Koehnline, the commanding officer of Headquarters and Services Battalion, about dropping the charges. Corporal Slaughter was a member of the Headquarters and Services Battalion. Colonel Koehnline's office was also next door to General Olson's office. I was given a polite cold shoulder when I attempted to explain the facts of the case. I was undeterred.

I wrote letters to Corporal Slaughter's former teachers, his minister, his parents, and his scout master to get affidavits attesting to his character. I also studied the lack of a simple, clear-cut operating procedure involving the use and maintenance of vehicles at FLC headquarters. In fact, in contrast to the rest of the motor pools on base, headquarters assumed an air of disdainful separation and followed its own methods any way that it pleased.

According to Corporal Slaughter, he admittedly presumed on his position when he took the chief of staff's vehicle without getting permission. He went out after hours on Highway 1. He claimed that he went on a preventive maintenance run, whereas the government alleged that he went out to drop a friend at a skivy house and to make a visit himself. There was evidence, however, that the former chief of staff of Brigadier General Olson had formulated an unofficial policy requiring the drivers to go out and test-drive repaired vehicles on Highway 1 as a part of vehicle maintenance.

Before Slaughter had been handpicked as the general's driver, he was a mechanic and served as an unofficial mechanic for the drivers at headquarters. Knowing this, the chief of staff's driver had approached him earlier in the week and asked him to take his vehicle out on the road sometime when he had an opportunity to check the front end and transmission. The corporal agreed to do so at the first opportunity. This turned out to be the evening of 2 June, when he was stopped.

The fly in the soup came when Slaughter was supposed to have stated to the road master when he was pulled over that, indeed, he was not out alone on the highway but that he was picking up a friend at a local hospitality house. This statement seemed to be corroborated by the fact that a Sergeant Leasher was also picked up in the village by the road master after he apprehended Slaughter.

Sergeant Leasher had been going with a Vietnamese girl who worked on the base, and her mother was visiting from Hue that night. The amorous sergeant wanted to take advantage of this opportunity to talk to his future mother-in-law about a marriage contract. Before leaving the base, Sergeant Leasher approached Slaughter, who worked nearby at headquarters. Knowing something about the procedures for after-hours maintenance runs, Leasher asked whether Slaughter was going to make a run that night, and, if so, would he mind picking him up on the way back to the base. Slaughter said he was not sure that he would be going out that night, and nothing further was said between them.

Later, Slaughter drove out on the highway and was stopped, alone, going in the opposite direction on the highway for a maintenance run. The road master apparently had word that he was out on an unauthorized run and that he supposedly had taken Sergeant Leasher with him. The road master and Slaughter had had words before, and he asked Slaughter where Leasher was and, specifically, whether he was in a scivy house. Corporal Slaughter replied that the sergeant was not in a scivy house but rather at his girlfriend's house and that he was not involved. Nevertheless, the road master gave him the alternative of either picking up Leasher or going back to the dispatch shack, where the road master would call the MPs. They would go through the village house by house until they found the man. Slaughter was thus persuaded to go pick Leasher up, and they were then both run in and charged.

After the court heard the testimony, they decided that Slaughter did not intend to misappropriate the government vehicle because he thought he was on official duty for a preventive maintenance run. The prosecution was not able to prove beyond a reasonable doubt that he violated the curfew because he honestly thought he was on official business. He was acquitted on every charge.

I could not help but be amused over the killing glares that the chief of staff's secretary gave to Slaughter when the secretary testified. He swore that no general's driver was ever authorized to take a vehicle of the chief's without either his expressed approval or that of the aide; he just could not show that the drivers were told this.

As part of the command's unofficial intent to hang Corporal Slaughter legally, they kept him in the country beyond the expiration of his tour for more than a month (he had previously extended for six months as well) and put him to work in the police shed under a lance corporal. Still, I learned an obvious but profound lesson in defending Corporal Slaughter. On his way home he stopped by to thank me for my efforts and added, "We really pulled one over on them, didn't we, sir?" He then admitted that he had taken the chief of staff's jeep out to see a girl himself and that he also planned to stop at another house and pick up Sergeant Leasher. He had lied to me and to the court. I told him to get out of my sight. I now realize that when he said, "I didn't do it, sir," that I had confused his apparent sincerity that he was innocent for his sincere desire to escape punishment.

6 / Summer 1968—Bracing for the Enemy's "Third Wave" Offensive

24 July 1968

It has now been two days, but the time blows by so quickly I seem to lose track. We experienced two rocket attacks at FLC that resulted in four killed and thirty-nine injured. Many of those injured, I understand, are from bunker injuries that happened when people ran from their huts through walls, stumped their toes, and so on. The Army unit next to us suffered two dead and some thirty wounded, and the Navy Seabees camp on the beach took one dead and two wounded. Two of our dead and nineteen of our wounded came when a bunker took a direct hit, exploding it like a deck of cards. When the attack began, everyone in that immediate area ran to that unlucky bunker, and there was a hundred-to-one chance that it would be hit. Another of our dead was killed on perimeter defense, and the fourth was killed by the accidental discharge of one of our own mortars. He was part of a motor crew firing illumination rounds when one of the rounds dropped in the tube had a hang fire. The crew kicked the tube and waited a minute to let it cool and then tilted it to let the round slide out of the tube where it could be disarmed. When the tube was tilted, it was so hot that the gunner could not hold it. Then, as he was letting it back down to the ground, he carelessly put his head over the barrel when the round cooked off. The shell took half of his head off.

Apparently, most, if not all, of our fatalities have come from head wounds. People peek out to see what is happening and take a big chunk of shrapnel between the ears, or when the rounds begin to detonate, they start running instead of hitting the ground and are cut down.

We received intelligence reports last night that the NVA and VC are ready to launch their long-awaited new offensive and that we should expect new attacks, but nothing has materialized as yet. The prevalent mood is pregnant with expectation, and I have used the time to have every man get his gear into shape and draw ammunition and pyrotechnics and to accelerate our training. Yesterday, I drove around in a jeep getting a firsthand view of the different designated penetration points that my company could be ordered to react to and familiarizing myself with the terrain. Going along the road, I passed long convoys of trucks, armored cars, and tanks. The Army of the Republic of Vietnam (ARVN) camps were beehives of activity as they prepared for the attack. I drove out to the various combined action units in our tactical area of responsibility to gauge their ability to hold out and how best I could react to their defense. For the first time, I noticed many of the children were not laughing and waving at us but were frowning; some even threw small rocks.

We drove over to First Marine Division, where I had an excellent briefing. Captured documents show the enemy objective to be Da Nang, which is the most important U.S./ARVN center in I Corps and the supply, command, and troop and communication center of this area. The enemy has plans for a twofold attack. First, they want to start their attack with sapper assaults by trained demolition experts on major installations in the city and around the air base, which are, second, to be followed by infantry attacks from NVA units, who will infiltrate the city and occupy key positions similar to the prior Tet attacks in Hue and Saigon. Their objectives include rendering the air base inoperable and occupying and destroying large areas of the dock facilities. They will mount attacks on the headquarters area of III Marine Amphibious Forces, the naval security administration headquarters, the town hall, the radio station, the main bridge, and the market area and then otherwise attempt to force a battle of destruction in the heart of the city. They have three possible approach routes; one is through the mountain passes from the west, another is out of the mountains to the southwest of the airfield, and the last is south down the coast through Ap Nam O village and FLC. If this third route turns out to be the case (but this seems unlikely to me), then our FLC Provisional Rifle Company will be part of the forces that will have to stop them.

We seem to be well enough prepared for this attack, but it will be next to impossible to keep at least some of them from infiltrating into the city.

In fact, at this moment the clouds are down on the deck, and rain is falling in thick, driving sheets. This is the time I would pick to begin an attack if I were a VC.

The other night when we were hit, I remember moving as if in a daze. It was 1:00 AM, and I had fallen into a deep sleep when I vaguely heard someone yelling "Incoming" and "Rockets." I heard the rockets screaming in, but for some reason, I thought that the rest of my friends in the hut were still asleep. I went from bed to bed to awaken them, but by this time I realized they had left a long time ago and that the explosions were getting louder and closer. Then I really woke up and ran outside to our newly completed bunker, when a thunderclap made the ground shake like jelly. The mess hall nearby had just been blown away. Within ten minutes the explosions moved away and died off completely. I was drained and did not feel excited or stimulated at all—only weary all over and conscious that I had not been touched. I put on my helmet, flak jacket, and so on and ran to the Combat Operations Center (COC) bunker to check on the situation and to muster the company in case we had to react. Inside the bunker were a mass of people marking plotting boards and giving orders against a background of ringing telephones. This is the nerve center of our operations and a vital installation in times of attack. Around 2:00 AM we had another attack, but this time it was shorter.

I enjoyed watching the command post in action and the opportunity to react with my Marines at the nearby ready tents. Organizing the people, I got them under cover and walked around, talking to them and checking on them to calm them down. I did not get any sleep the rest of the night and checked frequently on our patrols to be sure that they were not caught in the open and cut off. Thankfully, they came home safely, and the dawn eventually came uneasily, wet and cloudy. What the next few days will bring is uncertain.

25 July 1968

Last night near 7:00 PM I was in the Headquarters and Service Company (H&S Co.) office when rockets came thundering in and hit a nearby troop area. We all ducked and jumped for the bunker while the ground shivered from the impacts. Later, I found out that my company administrative chief, Staff Sergeant Moshier, was killed when the first rocket made a direct hit on his hut. He was a fine man, and I really feel down in the dumps over this. He had only a few days left in Vietnam and often joked that he slept with his tennis shoes on. He said that unless the first one hit him, he would be twenty feet underground before the dust cleared. When a man is blown to oblivion by a mine or a randomly fired rocket, his death seems so impersonal and futile. We now talk about the dead and dying so casually that it is almost as if they have only gone on leave. They are soon forgotten.

26 July 1968

Tonight we had another alert. The sirens sound now anytime someone in the Da Nang area is about to be hit. "Rockets! Rockets!" breaks in over the radio network when our outposts spot the glare of an incoming rocket. No one knows where it is going, so we all are alerted to go to ground. This time, the rockets hit the Da Nang airfield and trashed seven million dollars' worth of aircraft.

28 July 1968

The strain of the unknown in the anticipation of a major enemy offensive was reflected last night when two of our patrols fired on each other. The patrols were briefed before departing the perimeter as to their call signs, routes, and times of departure and estimated times of return to base. They left from different locations and at staggered times in order to keep the enemy off balance and to avoid running into each other in the dark. Unfortunately, once the first patrol departed, everything fell apart.

Both patrols were fully aware that enemy units could be active in our area and that there was a need to be on total alert. The first patrol to depart left two hours before the second patrol and was supposed to have moved through any areas the second patrol would cross long before the second patrol reached those areas. But flares from units of the Twenty-sixth Marines who operated near to us kept slowing the first patrol down. Each time another flare lit up the darkness, everyone froze until the flare drifted down and went out. As this went on, the first patrol fell further behind in its schedule and failed to keep the COC informed of its delays and its position. The two patrols were on a collision course.

Around 1:00 AM, automatic-rifle fire began, followed by garbled reports

Marines of the Provisional Rifle Company being briefed outside the Combat Operations Center, July 1968, before leaving on a sweep of hills overlooking Loc Hoa Pass.

from both patrols. I ran to the COC bunker and tried to find out what was going on. All I knew was that we had two patrols in contact with someone and that we had casualties. But it was soon clear that each patrol was in the same area. After identifying flares were fired off, it was clear that in the dark the patrols had crossed paths and instantly opened fire.

I later learned that the point man for the second patrol observed figures moving slowly in the flickering light of a dying flare. Knowing that no friendly units were supposed to be in the area, the patrol opened fire, wounding two Marines from the first patrol.

All this took place in a short space of time. As the men realized what had happened, there was shock and the need to evacuate the wounded. There was also the need to reorganize quickly and get both patrols moving again to complete their missions. This was not the type of situation I was trained to deal with at Quantico.

The latest intelligence now indicates that the enemy will be infiltrating small units of infantry and sappers into our tactical area of responsibility and south into Da Nang during the next few days. These units will next link up with other units that have already slipped into the city. Their plan is to attempt to take and hold key areas in the city for three days.

29 July 1968

I took out a patrol today to see whether we had any newcomers in our area. With flak jackets and helmets, plus weapons and full loads of ammo, we know it's a bitch to go out and hump paddies in this heat, but the men performed magnificently. They kept good security, and we swept a large distance, to no avail. It is amazing, however, how beautiful the countryside is when we move away from the camp perimeter. Yesterday, I took the patrol out to the farthest limits of our tactical area and explored some islands that dot the marshy rice paddies near the Song Cu De River. When we climbed up on them, it was like entering paradise. The breeze was fresh across the river and swept the heights constantly, while the aromatic smell of thick green grass was like perfume. There were tall old shade trees, and in a small glade, we came across nearly intact ruins of an old Buddhist temple with mosaic inlays of Chinese dragons. It seemed remotely peaceful and out of place. We rested while the war seemed remote and far away. The wind played in the green rice shoots of the fields around us and rustled the leaves of the ancient trees.

Later, as we were going through another village and stopped at a well for water, I noticed an elderly, worn-out-looking Vietnamese woman, her teeth dyed purple from beetle nut juice, watching me. I could only wonder whether she knew the difference between us and the young Frenchmen who had patrolled these same areas years earlier.

Although I wear no rank indication when I go on patrols, it does not seem to fool the local Vietnamese. As soon as we stop in a village, the adults as well as the children immediately know who is in charge. Today a mother brought her infant to me for medical treatment when I sat down for some water and a break. The child's head was a sickening, swollen mass of pus, and the two front lobes of his little head felt like sponges to the touch. I think this filth was the result of lice and no bathing. When the mother picks the scabs off the wound and washes the wound with putrid, foul well water, it only makes things worse. I put mercurochrome on the child's head and left the rest of the bottle with his mother, but it will not do any good.

Tom Loftis, one of my platoon commanders, is the civic affairs officer here at the base and tells me that time after time mothers bring their children to our children's hospital for treatment. They fearfully turn the child over to the nurses for treatment but want the youngster back that same day. Sometimes a child will be kept a few days until almost cured, then the mother will show up outside the camp gates, throwing herself onto the road, barbed wire, and the gates, crying and moaning for the return of the child. We have no alternative but to return the child, even though the youngster is not cured. A few days later, Tom says, after returning to the village, the baby again is a mass of pus from lack of sanitary conditions, but the mother is as happy as a pig in a pen.

We eventually stumbled out onto the highway on completion of our patrol and were nearly annihilated by swarms of Vietnamese roaring down the highway on their motor scooters out for a Sunday afternoon joyride. We patrol their filthy, backward, apathetic country while these pleasure-seeking people ride the gravy train. Why aren't they doing more for their own country? History, I hope, will recall our mission here as a noble one, but more and more, I am beginning to believe that Vietnam is not worth American lives. Of course, only time can tell whether we prevail or not and whether the sacrifice is worthwhile.

About a week ago, our legal office was invited to the nearby Seabees' camp for steak and beer. The Seabees are the famed construction units of the Navy, and they have a knack for living well. They have built an officers' club on the beach that could be more expected in some South Seas island paradise. It is circular and open, with thatched leaves for the roof. The view at night of the twinkling lights from the vessels bobbing gently in the bay is beautiful to behold. There are high mountains on either side of the bay, and the lights of our camps can be seen sparkling through the evening haze. The beaches and scenery here could equal any tourist areas in the world if it were not for the war.

30 July 1968

The day after tomorrow I have orders to go to Japan for three days to take testimony from Lance Corporal Timms, who is paraplegic from the .45 gunshot wound. It will be a welcomed chance to travel and break out of my routine at FLC, but I wish that this trip was under different circumstances.

Last night we had a USO show with a group of traveling Australians called the "Southlanders." They were tremendous. They were quick and funny and could sing and play their instruments well and, above all, had a cute blonde for the troops' morale. I think I was transfixed during her songs, looking in awe at her blue eyes, her long blonde hair, and her graceful body. Lord God, what a delight! It was delicious to be able to lose oneself for several hours and be entertained.

Today, we received a new second lieutenant straight from the States as a new lawyer. We all were ecstatic. Dennis Sims went around like a mother hen, making sure that he was issued a flak jacket and helmet and knew where a bunker was located. We all looked at him like a new pet puppy. This means that some of our caseload will ease for a change.

I drove into downtown Da Nang this afternoon to naval headquarters, where I talked to authorities about two of my clients who have been charged with possession of marijuana. I hoped to persuade them to try the two by a special court-martial instead of by a general court—no such luck.

Downtown Da Nang, especially the residential section, has a quaint atmosphere that still lingers from the French years. The riverfront, with its barges and boats, reminds me of the Seine in Paris, and I am sure it must once have been graced by little sidewalk cafes and shops. Today, however, there are armed soldiers at every corner, barbed wire across the once-beautiful walls and lawns, bunkers where cafes once stood, and the putrid smell of garbage in the streets that is so common to Vietnam. Nevertheless, there is still just a hint of past beauty, an echo of French voices in the signs and monuments, and perhaps a whispering memory of the anxieties breathed in years gone by, when at another time the Communist Viet Minh moved their forces on Da Nang.

A Marine sergeant who is on his third tour here tells me that he is impressed with the progress that has been made in turning the city into a fortified camp. When he was here two years ago, there was no concertina wire wrapped around buildings and strung along the tops of fences; no bunkers bristling with automatic weapons that brooded silently down the wide avenues; and no troops and civil police at every corner. All this has now changed. I can only hope Da Nang will be spared the full horrors of war that have washed over Hue and Saigon.

14 August 1968

Despite high hopes and dreams of geisha girls and Tokyo at night, I never made it to Japan. My trip was canceled when my group reached Okinawa. First Lieutenant Pete Mastaglio, one of my fellow lawyers, Corporal Rassler,

A residential area with checkpoints in downtown Da Nang.

a court reporter, and I set out at the crack of dawn on 1 August for Japan via Okinawa. We waited around for a flight out of the transient terminal and finally caught a hop on a C-130 transport at 11:30 AM. Five hours later we bumped, shuddered, and heaved our way into Okinawa. It was beautiful. The island that a bare two months earlier had seemed so dirty now appeared like a lush tropical paradise. Everything is relative. It was so grand to be able to relax and not have to worry about rockets or anything more serious than what drink I planned to order next. Major Hall, an ex-college wrestling star with a fine sense of humor as well as a quick mind, was with us also. We went to an Okinawa restaurant for dinner after checking in and managed to be loud and happily obnoxious. We repulsed everyone before lurching out to find a hot-tub bath. Then, for $2.00 I managed to get wrung out in a steam bath, which was followed by a massage. Later, we took off for the bars and strip palaces to admire the local talent and cheer them on to bigger and greater spectacles. That night I had the first deep sleep I had known in two months.

In Vietnam, my body and senses fight going to sleep. It is only reluctantly that the mind lets itself relax and becomes unconscious. There is a feeling of being naked and letting one's guard down as one drifts into sleep. This was not the case in Okinawa, and even the B-52s taking off on raids to Vietnam did not bother me. Thus, my twenty-sixth birthday passed.

The next day dawned even more beautiful than the last. We had a late, leisurely breakfast and then drove over to enjoy the Army golf course. The fairways are in a setting that has few equals. At one point, a person can tee off and from his high position look down to the bay, watch the ships on one side of the island, catch up with his ball, and then putt in onto a green where he can look out to the ocean off the opposite side of the island. It is as if there was not a war. One sees families and American cars, movies, and restaurants ("O" clubs—which we were not allowed into because we did not have a coat and tie), and one has to get used to paying American prices again.

That afternoon we packed our gear, picked up our orders, and went whistling off to the terminal to catch our flight to Japan. Ten minutes prior to takeoff, I was paged and told that a light colonel had called to say that we were not to go to Japan, that our orders had been changed, and that I was to call him. Hell! I fumbled to find this upstart's name who dared do this to us and called everywhere to find him. I finally caught him at home; he was having supper. His daughter called him to the phone. He informed me that Lance Corporal Timms, the man we were going to interview, had already been medivaced back to the States, so there was no reason to go. We stayed in Okinawa another day; it rained all day, and that afternoon there was an earthquake that registered a magnitude of 4 on the Richter scale.

Ultimately I worked out a pretrial agreement in Lance Corporal Kerr's case. Although the shooting was tragic, it was accidental, and Kerr had an excellent record otherwise. Because my boss at the FLC legal office, Lieutenant Colonel Haden, wanted the boy to go to jail and would not approve a pretrial agreement, I forwarded my proposal to General Olson. The general not only approved my pretrial agreement but also knocked four months off the sentence. Lance Corporal Kerr received a four-month suspended sentence and was reduced in rank to private first class.

In the meantime, I returned to work full time, getting ready for two cases involving two Seabees, Jim Thomas and Jay Fulton. These men were charged with the possession and use of marijuana and the larceny of stealing cement bags to trade for it. As their cases progressed, they dropped by to see me nearly every day. The office scuttlebutt placed bets that I would soon have to draw up adoption papers on them. Jerry Cunningham claimed that when they came to the office to ask for me they asked for "Daddy."

My case had a twofold plan. First, I hoped to keep out the evidence against them by knocking holes in the government's chain of custody, and then, second, I planned to argue a defense based on a theory of entrapment. I arranged separate trials for them, with a general court-martial for Fulton on Monday and Thomas's court the next day.

Fulton's case went from 9:00 AM to 11:30 PM. I spent all morning trying to keep the marijuana cigarettes from being admitted into evidence. I objected to any and everything that was possible. We fought over every issue and hashed out every fact. I cross-examined the government's main witness and tried to destroy his credibility. I dragged out all the dirty linen. I tried to show that the government witness had a drinking problem; that he had few friends and little respect from anyone at the Seabees' base; that he smoked marijuana; and that he tried to push it off on others at the camp so as to entrap them; and so on. But it did not do any good. I did my best, but the court chose to disbelieve my client and to believe the government's witness. This meant, then, that all my efforts to impeach the government's witness bounced back against me. When the court finally came in with its verdict, Jay Fulton received two years at hard labor and a bad-conduct discharge. I was floored at such a stiff penalty.

The main thing that I remember from this trial was the outstanding job done by the law officer, Colonel John De Barr. He commands the Navy–Marine Corps judicial activity office in I Corps. He and I were the only Marines in the courtroom. The accused, the court members, and the government counsel were all from the Navy. The colonel is a distinguished, fine gentleman, a former infantry platoon commander on Iwo Jima, and a true scholar of the law; moreover, he seemed to go out of his way to grant my objections and to overrule the other side's. He congratulated me later on my efforts, which I appreciated.

The following day I picked up my next client for trial and found a very agitated young man. When Thomas learned that Fulton received two years and a bad-conduct discharge, he walked outside his hooch and threw up. I told him that when Jay was tried yesterday, he had been tried also and that now he should plead guilty. It was a hard choice, but I believed it was in his best interest. At times like this, a lawyer has to trust his own judgment, and this is when the burden feels heaviest on my shoulders. Jim Thomas pled guilty, and I stressed to the court the good prior record of the accused. I emphasized his

Purple Heart, his refusal to be medivaced, and his desire to return to combat duty. I referred to his family history and his future plans for college and marriage, and I reminded the court members as forcibly as I could that due to Thomas's admitted mistake, the court had the power to either ruin any future he had dreamed about or give him another chance. He was sentenced to only six months at hard labor and no bad-conduct discharge.

We have had a considerable lull in enemy action for the last two weeks. According to intelligence, the enemy did try to get an offensive off the ground on the twenty-third of July but was unable to make it work. The target is still Da Nang, but apparently the enemy battalions and regiments are now assembling to the south of the city in the valleys and islands there. The NVA have an entire corps in the Da Nang area, but I doubt they can take the city. They have already lost one-third of their sapper units and many of their local VC guides. Apparently, they will try to infiltrate the city and hope to draw off our infantry units by rocketing isolated areas, such as FLC and district capitals, hoping we will then commit units to sweeping operations to locate their rocket battalions and leave holes in our lines.

Sappers could hit us easily and get into the camp to do a great deal of damage if they wanted to. Apparently, no units in the area have been able to detect the VC sappers until after they first penetrated the protective barbed wire and were inside our positions. They are said to take up to four hours to crawl the last one hundred yards and are stripped down to shorts and are smeared with black grease for camouflage.

Our intelligence tells us that the NVA could be into their strategic reserves now. We have killed soldiers from Ho Chi Min's palace guard. Intelligence also reports that knapsacks from fifty of their dead were lined up, and each one had a full set of freshly pressed utilities in it, with toothbrush, toothpaste, and mirrors in exactly the same place in each knapsack. These are first-rate troops, but I cannot imagine why they are down here in our area unless the enemy is desperate for a victory and is committing the best remaining troops for this battle.

Our intelligence also indicates that the enemy will start its attack on Da Nang by attacking the outlying hamlets and bases with rockets and mortars in an effort to throw us off guard, disperse our forces, and intimidate the people into cowed submission so that our information sources will dry up at this critical moment. Then they will strike inside the city. We are told that the enemy commanders will be receiving their orders to march within the next five days and that FLC could be hit any time now. If by some chance the attack again fails to materialize, then the enemy is expected to hit the hamlets and refugee camps and step up their program of political assassinations and kidnapping. We can only wait and see.

I have received birthday cards and letters from all my family, and they really mean a great deal to me, especially those from Bill, my older brother. I guess this is the first time I have ever known him to say openly that he is proud of me. This touches me very deeply.

17 August 1968

The rains are on us now, with low-lying clouds wrapping the mountains in a spray of white. We are expecting the enemy to make some move by the nineteenth, which is a Viet Cong holiday. Last night I was in the COC when a report came in that the point man on one of my patrols had been attacked. He was moving along a trail when suddenly out of the dark a water buffalo charged him, knocking him head over heels and breaking his nose. He fired his M-79 point blank at the beast, but the projectile did not explode because the target was too close for it to arm itself. Another member of a patrol yesterday afternoon had a piece of luck. He stepped on a trip wire leading to a Chicom grenade, but it failed to detonate. The patrol blew it in place. This young Marine is lucky to still be in one piece.

A brief description of the people whom I am working with in our legal shop is in order. There is the brilliant Jim Haydel, known as "His Magnificence"; the office humorist, Jerry Cunningham from Tennessee (who says daily, "If you hate Vietnam, wear green!"); 6′5″, 230-pound Pete Mastaglio from Long Island, New York, called "Lurch," who is a fine man in every sense of the word; Dennis Sims, the fabulous "Kung Fu" from Colorado, who has an engaging personality and more courtroom common sense than any of the rest of us; Ron Williamson, "Little Round Mound," a lawyer and our legal assistance officer, who tends to be deliberate and methodical but is delightful company; Tom Schwindt—"Lightning"; John Reilly, "Snoopy"; and many others, but it is late, and I am too tired to continue.

Fellow lawyers at Force Logistics Command legal office: *(left to right)* Jim Haydel, Bob Wachsmuth, Pete Mastaglio, Dennis Sims, Mike Murray, and Jerry Cunningham.

20 August 1968

I have just received a call from one of my friends from The Basic School who is now at the I Corps Bridge in Da Nang as an MP officer. He told me that Terry Hale, from Abilene, Texas, and my suitemate when I was at Quantico last year, has been killed in action. What a shame. Terry was a tall, awkward-looking, red-headed boy with a crew cut who was always ready to help out someone who at the last minute was rushing to get his gear together for an inspection. He was the one who was always chosen when a job had to be done and it was important to have someone who could absolutely be depended on. He had been a physical education major and a trainer at the University of Texas with the football team and loved to talk about his school. He was more than a boy, yet a young man with more than a trace remaining of his teenage years; he was full of promise, clean and honorable. I went home with him last Christmas from Washington, D.C. We had three days' leave by the grace of the Marine Corps, but flights were delayed, and we missed our connection from Dallas into Abilene. I remember how we were both upset at missing the plane, happy to be back in Texas, and impatient to get home, so we rented a car and drove all night. Terry paid for it until I could repay him later. We talked for hours as the cold was locked out of the automobile roaring down the frigid deserted highway. We pulled into his house around 3:30 AM. His parents quickly got out of bed and, with his little sister, came down to fix breakfast for their wonderful boy and his new friend. They were so proud of him, and he gleamed with pride in turn. I stayed for coffee and then rushed on home myself. He was their only son, adopted. And now he is a beautiful memory, a sacrifice too splendid, too dear for anyone other than parents to appreciate.

I have also learned that Bill Green, my friend from Boston with whom I spent Thanksgiving, has been sent home already with three wounds. Skip Howland from Nashville died ten days after arriving. I do not mean to dwell on unpleasant events, but the members of Second Platoon, Charlie Company, that I grew to know and respect during five months of The Basic School are in the war.

Last night, while in the COC bunker, we received an intelligence report that FLC was due to be rocketed between 2:00 and 3:00 AM. I went back to my bed and lay down while wild thoughts ran through my mind as I imagined NVA gunners traversing and elevating some distant mechanism so that they could drop their first round precisely on Don Griffis. Then, after a restless sleep, I saw the gray smear of dawn arrive.

Intelligence also indicates that the NVA and VC are building up massive stockpiles of captured ARVN and U.S. uniforms and equipment to use in the coming offensive. They intend to infiltrate Da Nang so disguised and cause havoc. They are slow in getting their "Third Wave" off the ground and have had many setbacks. If it is completely crushed and they take heavy casualties, then their will to fight, at least to fight conventional battles, should be set back considerably.

21 August 1968

Yesterday I had a special court-martial where I represented a character named Blanchard. He already had a suspended bad-conduct discharge from his last trial, has had three trials in the past, as well as six office hours (a procedure for limited punishment from an individual's commanding officer), and has been in the brig his last six months here. He is not a bad fellow really, just a real goofus. It just so happened that his trial took place the morning after "Buster" Cherry had been up until 4:00 AM trying to make his point in a craps game but succeeded only in losing $50 and getting trashed on beer. Chuck Cherry is also alias the "King of the Underworld" because he inhabits our bunker at night instead of sleeping in the hooch. We pulled him out of the bowels of the earth in time to make it up to the courtroom, where he was to act as president of the court.

Blanchard was at risk for a bad-conduct discharge and another six months' confinement at hard labor. The confinement and forfeitures of pay were the desires of the command because if they merely wanted a bad-conduct discharge, all they had to do was vacate his prior suspended bad-conduct discharge without a trial. My client wanted a bad-conduct discharge and to be ordered out of the service before he got into any more trouble, but became pale at the thought of going back to the brig.

The trial lacked some of the exalted atmosphere that usually cloaks these affairs. When Buster swore in Pete Mastaglio as trial counsel and me as defense counsel, he was visibly swaying on his feet, and I had visions of his blowing lunch all over the courtroom while the court reporter tried to record it all ("Say again, sir?"). Despite his setbacks, Buster rallied and proceeded into the trial, only to go through the dry heaves when I put my boy on the stand to testify. Of the other two members on the court, one had served as my assistant defense counsel in a past case, and the other one slept through the proceedings. My boy, despite the fact he was inherently dumb, began to perceive that all was not well in the courtroom. In fact, he began to see visions of a long stretch behind wire when my questions were obviously having little effect on the one sleeping member or on poor miserable Buster.

We came back in for the sentence, and it was a bad-conduct discharge without brig time or forfeitures. Blanchard skated. He expressed his animal pleasure at the outcome and was led off by the brig chaser. Blanchard, as I have said, is not a bad person; he just has the habit of stealing the CO's jeep and driving off into town and the off-limits areas. It became so regular that if the CO was ever missing his vehicle or it was late, he immediately called to find out where Blanchard was.

Pete Mastaglio was the only one not satisfied with the verdict. He kept asking Buster how in the world anyone could bring back such a ridiculous verdict, but Buster would only assume a meditative, all-knowing air and say that after losing $50 the night before at craps he did not feel inclined to work forfeitures on anyone.

We joke with Buster now and tell him he had better write his wife to mortgage the house, start sewing her own clothes, and put the baby on Dim Rats (diminished rations). He has squandered all their money in Vietnam.

There was another disturbance last night from down in the bunker. Kung Fu (Dennis Sims) and Jerry Cunningham have now moved in with Buster. They are short-timers, and no one wants to be knocked off at the last. Around 4:00 AM, Dennis shook Jerry and whispered, "Don't move, don't make a sound. The whole bunker is quivering like jelly!" Jerry was terrified, being aroused in this matter, and turned on the light, expecting to see the bunker cave in on them under the impact of a devastating artillery barrage. An electric fan was on the floor, and it was causing the floor under Sims's cot to shake. Later, Jerry was again awakened as Dennis rolled over and stuck his feet into the fan. Neither one of them looked particularly rested this morning.

22 August 1968

Last night we went on 100 percent alert as of 6:00 PM as we again braced for the much-talked-about, long-awaited "Third Wave" by the enemy. Earlier that morning at headquarters, we were told that an attack was "imminent" (we were told so again this morning), and yesterday evening we went into Condition II, which means an attack is expected any moment. I gathered the company, issued ammunition, inspected the men, and readied myself for at least a rocket attack and corresponding mortar and sapper attacks with infantry probes as accompaniment, but, as usual, when we expected it the most, nothing happened.

23 August 1968

The enemy offensive began last night at 3:00 AM as far as we were concerned. I think my reflexes are better now. I was sound asleep and the next moment rolled out of my rack and crashed to the ground, crawling out of the door for the bunker. The first round that hit us triggered something deep in the back of my mind like an automatic switch. The air was alive with the sound of in-

coming rounds, both mortars and rockets, under a sickly yellowish sky illuminated by flares. It took awhile, but then I noticed a new sound—automatic-
weapon fire on the perimeter. I was sure sappers were loose in the compound
and we were under infantry attack, but it turned out that we were only being
probed. Still, VC came up within 100 to 150 meters of our perimeter to fire
their version of the bazooka at our bunkers and dropped their mortar rounds
into our perimeter as well as the Army's and Seabees' perimeters nearby.
They apparently were after the helicopters at the Army base and fired more
than 150 rounds at them. Fortunately, most of the rounds shot at FLC fell
short and hit outside the barbed wire of our perimeter. We were hit twice
more during the night, as were other bases throughout the Da Nang area.

By morning it became apparent that the enemy offensive had finally begun. Enemies were on the bridges, and gunships were being called in on
them. By noon apparently two VC sapper battalions had been committed to
get inside Da Nang. Gunfire is everywhere in the Da Nang area.

The enemy may try to take Ap Nam O village to the north of us tonight. If
they do, we will have to retake it. I guess I feel that it is a relief that the enemy
offensive has finally started, and I hope we can hurt him seriously enough to
shorten the war. I know my enthusiasm and morale have never been higher.
There is something about the bigness of the situation, the uncertainty, and
the danger that makes my blood pound, and life seems keener.

26 August 1968

I have managed to stumble through the last few days with dwindling sleep
and confused disgust. The enemy has never solidly committed himself anywhere and now appears to be disengaging three battalions to the south of
Da Nang with plans to link them up with other units operating to the west
of the city and then try to force the passes in that area. This would bring
them close to our area of responsibility, and we will have to watch for the
enemy's possible move on Ap Nam O. In the meantime, intelligence reports
(which are rarely accurate but eagerly accepted) indicate that Charlie will
try to break into Da Nang tonight.

We have not been hit since the night of August 23, but then neither
have many other units. There have been hard attacks in isolated portions of
the Da Nang southern perimeter, but they were obviously only probes. By

word of mouth, I have heard of hand-to-hand fighting on Monkey Mountain when the VC tried to storm the Marine positions. One lieutenant was coming out of his hut carrying his .45 when he bumped into a VC carrying an AK-47. The lieutenant blew the top of the VC's head off with his pistol. Another group of Marines cornered two VC in the washroom, where one was wounded and captured and the other blew himself to Buddha with a grenade. A friend of mine said he saw an Amtrak going through downtown Da Nang when a young Vietnamese girl ran out on the sidewalk and fired a rocket launcher at it point-blank, turning it into a burning, exploding wreck. The ARVN soldiers captured her immediately, pulled her into the center of the street, stripped her clothes off, and executed her on the spot, but all this is hearsay.

I do know that the Seventh Engineers' road, a dirt road that runs along the southwest part of our perimeter, has now been closed due to recent mining incidents. In two days, a dump truck and two jeeps, both FLC vehicles, have been smashed to pieces and thrown on their sides, killing or wounding their occupants.

30 August 1968

The action flared up three nights ago and again two nights ago, but it was relatively quiet last night. Three nights ago Combined Action Platoon (CAP) 282 was subjected to heavy mortar and small-arms fire. Combined Action Platoon 282 is only a few miles from FLC and is manned by some South Vietnamese PF troops. I could clearly see the entire action from the crow's nest high on top of the COC bunker. There were constant "crumps" as mortars impacted in the darkness, along with flashes from the .50-caliber machine gun as it seemed to slowly spit its red tracers out into the nearby hills and the quicker hammering of the light automatic weapons. Flares lighted the surrounding scene, with green ones marking the location of the South Vietnamese PF troops and red flares indicating to the besieged PF group where to shift their fire. To a casual observer, it looked like a hell of a fight and seemed as if an attempt was being made to overrun the unit, but the attack lasted too long. The VC carefully rehearse and prepare their attacks, hit fast, and then clear out, never going much over ten minutes. What really appears to have happened now is that the VC wanted to run some supplies

Chuck Cherry pondering the damage to his office after it was mortared the night of 29 August 1968.

through the valley and past the CAP unit. The VC set up a diversion that panicked the ARVN PF troops into running into their compound and firing their final protective fires while refusing to patrol for the enemy. They fired off nearly all the ammo they had in the camp and were neatly bottled up while the VC moved their goods through at will.

The night before last we were hit with ten 122 mm rockets at 7:55 PM, which killed one man and wounded three others. They impacted generally in the enlisted men's living area and caused the damage there. The ones who were hurt were apparently already in their bunker, but it was shoddily built, with chinks open in the side. A tiny piece of shrapnel entered and hit the Marine in the back of the head, killing him. I was in the COC working on patrol routes when we heard the first muffled explosion outside in the distance. We immediately rang the siren alarm and then monitored the casualty reports as they were given. I was very impressed at how quickly the men

from the Army helicopter pad from across the highway called over and offered their services to medivac our wounded. They are very helpful and are
a credit to the service.

Later that night, about 1:00 AM, we were hit by thirty to fifty mortar
rounds. One round hit next to our legal office, riddling one side with shrapnel
and nearly destroying two offices. Another round hit the chapel, and the
others hit near the enlisted men's club and area. Two officers and eight enlisted men were wounded, but none seriously, so we skated. The fact that we
are being hit by mortars means that Charlie is only 3,000 meters at maximum
from the center of our compound but probably is much closer. The patrol that
was out that night could clearly hear the rounds being dropped down the
tube as quickly as the VC gunners could load and fire them, but counter-
battery fire and helicopter gunships made them go to ground. I cannot really
estimate how many VC are in the area or what their intentions are, but I suspect they are trying to filter through our area and into Da Nang under the
cover of these attacks. Our patrols are better trained and more aggressive now
but have to do a better job preventing or disrupting these attacks.

2 September 1968

Back to Phu Bai. I flew north to Phu Bai the day before yesterday to interview witnesses for trial. When I stepped from the transport, a big man came
over and in a deep voice said, "Captain, don't I know you from somewhere?"
His name tag read "Cato." "D. G. Cato?" I asked. "That's right," he replied.
He had been my drill instructor at Quantico in the summer of 1963.

D. G. Cato, now a first lieutenant, still reminds me of Ernest Hemingway
in his appearance. In 1963, he was the drill instructor for my training platoon and set the example on how a staff noncommissioned officer should perform. He was superb, and we would have followed him anywhere. His positive leadership kept a group of officer candidates, most of whom were Texans,
from a near riot. The new second lieutenant assigned to our platoon was from
the University of Pennsylvania and came across as an arrogant jerk. In boot
camp, the drill instructor normally has the role of the heavy, and the lieutenant is the remote good guy. It became reversed in our case, and because
of this I think that Cato became special to the young men in our platoon.

He obviously kept up with many who had graduated from his old training platoon and recounted with pleasure how he had recently seen Don Higginbotham (another attorney in our platoon at boot camp) riding on the back of a tank in the DMZ while directing fire on enemy positions.

Five years later I next see him in Vietnam and as an officer. Even more unusual is that the case I am to try is a rehearing. My client was convicted the first time, but due to improper instructions by the president of the court, the case was thrown out. The prosecuting counsel who won the case was Cato.

Pete Mastaglio and I are here together. Pete will act as the government counsel, and after the trial we both are to give lectures on the duties and problems of trial and defense lawyers. Pete says he has found his main problem as prosecuting attorney to be acquittals; mine is convincing the court members to believe the defense counsel!

Pete is the butt of a lot of our practical jokes; because he is so big, it is like baiting a bear. Three days ago the civil affairs officer, whose office is next door to FLC legal, had a little porker that had come in through our wire during the night, and a group of us grabbed it. Although Pete was in talking to Major Moore, I called him out and told him that he had a client waiting for him in his office. When he went to his office, everyone went limp with laughter at the look on Pete's face as he stared at this pig that was seated in his office, oinking at him.

3 September 1968

We ran Private Smith's trial yesterday, and it took all day. Smith was convicted of assault with a deadly weapon for trying to cut a young lance corporal in half with a machete and was sentenced to four months' confinement and a bad-conduct discharge. I tried to raise a reasonable doubt that it was not Smith who swung the weapon and that it might not have been a machete that, in fact, was seen. Smith denied he was guilty, and a group of his buddies testified for him. In contrast, there was positive identification by four other witnesses besides the defendant that Smith did swing the blade and that, but for a warning, he would have killed Lance Corporal Donnahue.

Smith is a harmless-looking individual, and I am still puzzled as to why he would commit such an act when he did not know the lance corporal or

Peter and the pig. Pete is on the left.

have an apparent motive. Nevertheless, he was found guilty, and later the legal officer at Phu Bai told me that a number of other people saw Smith take the swing but did not want to testify because they were due to rotate home and did not want to be put on legal hold. Anyway, I did my best and even introduced an old axe handle into evidence to try to raise a doubt about what weapon was actually used. No soap. As Dennis Sims said, this case was lost when Smith took the machete and tried to subdivide the lance corporal.

Last night, we paid a visit to the Phu Bai officers' club. Dennis, Pete, and I started out rolling dice for drinks, but this rapidly degenerated. I remember walking outside and ordering drinks for everyone, but heaven knows who paid for them. I was broke. This morning I woke up with what tasted like a dead rat in my mouth, hot and cold chills, and a stomach that felt like it was in an advanced state of decay. I had to give a lecture at 8:00 AM on the duties of a defense counsel, but I do not think I impressed anyone.

At 9:30 or 10:00 AM, I began to rally, and we caught a ride with Ernie Cato into Hue to see where the fighting took place during last February's Tet offensive. We drove through the walled city into the citadel and the old Imperial Palace. It must have been beautiful once, but now there are ruins and shell holes everywhere. There are broad avenues in Hue, and the city seems

Pete Mastaglio on 3 September 1968 at the former Imperial Palace at Hue.

cleaner, less crowded, and more civilized than Da Nang. The palace grounds are still beautiful, with the Chinese dragons sculptured in the mosaics and carvings, large old bronze bells, nineteenth-century cannons, sunken gardens, moats around the thick palace walls, and many beautifully built and decorated temples and buildings. The palace grounds are basically deserted now while repairs are going forward, although they are made only slowly. Being there was like being at the ruins of a once-great civilization, and for the first time, I felt some sense of the nation that Vietnam must have been.

4 September 1968

Yesterday when I returned I discovered that during the night the Army compound had come under heavy mortar attack. The night combat patrol happened to be in the vicinity of the enemy mortar crew at the time and immediately took it under automatic-weapons and M-79 fire, causing them to break off the action and withdraw. At first light, Third Platoon swept the area and found nothing; however, reports from the villagers at Ap Trung Son said fifteen wounded VC were carried through their hamlet earlier that morning. I am very proud of the men. Whether they actually wounded that

D. G. Cato, my former drill instructor, at the former Imperial Palace at Hue.

many is really immaterial to me. As long as the villagers *think* we knocked heads that hard and as long as my men *think* their aggressiveness paid off so well, then the purpose has been served of cowing the locals and giving my people a tremendous boost in morale. It is beautiful how Marines react to combat. I looked at the patrol leader's after-action report, and in the space for "condition of patrol" was scrawled "tired but happy."

7 / Typhoon Bess Meets the Chaplain

9 September 1968

For three days beginning on the fourth of September, Typhoon Bess battered FLC. Gale winds reached up to sixty knots at a time, tin roofs were torn off, buildings were flooded, and rain swirled in sheets that felt like pinpricks when they hit the skin. We had to close the office one day due to flooding and the loss of electricity and a part of the roof. So we all splashed back to our huts to rack out. There was so much banging and wind noise and roaring of rain on the tin roof that I slept fitfully for two nights, thinking I would not be able to hear the explosions if Charlie tried to sneak in and hit us. I guess the storm proved that VC disliked being soaked like drowning rats as much as Marines.

An interesting sidelight to the typhoon has been the reaction of Chaplain George Kouvelis, the command chaplain, who rates a book to himself. He is a balding, eccentric, rather nondescript-looking individual full of the strengths and frailties of us all, but leaving something to be desired as a man of the cloth. For one thing, he is the butt of much ridicule at FLC, being referred to as "Zorba the Greek" because of his Greek surname. The higher command is especially incensed over the fortresslike bunker that he has had many Marines and Seabees build for him and that resembles a pyramid of Egypt. He has obtained huge logs and hundreds of sandbags and has used many laborers, who have spent hundreds of working hours to build a massive fortress that should withstand even a direct hit by a 122 mm rocket. To rationalize this waste of valuable resources and effort, he at first argued that the bunker would be available for the troops if an attack occurred and any were exposed in the nearby vicinity. Unfortunately, despite the gargantuan size of the beast, it will accommodate only eight people, that is, Father Kouvelis and his retinue. The chaplain is now more candid and admits that he built the bunker because he wants to live and he hates rocket attacks, which I find to be unimpeachable reasoning. He also has an answer to the chief of staff and other members of General Olson's staff who are openly hostile to him and accuse him of lack of faith. He says he has as much faith as the next man, but he does not see them standing around the streets demonstrating their bravery when we catch incoming.

The command, led by the chief of staff, ridiculed Father Kouvelis for his waste of material and the expense, but he stood up to them and said he would build what he liked. He now claims that of the one-hundred-plus heavy beams he acquired for construction, he gave more than seventy away to the troops when they could not obtain any from their own command. Matters have come to a head since the typhoon struck, however. Zorba was drowned out of his bunker like a fat cat and has been pumping water furiously from it ever since. This past Sunday, he had another one of his puzzling, inane sermons and told his flock that he did not know how to start the pump but that somehow, miraculously, it began to operate and throw the water out of his sanctuary. This was not exactly an inspiring message of faith for me, and I hope that the bilge pumps work better in heaven.

8 / Patrols and Alarms

17 September 1968

Yesterday I accompanied a patrol through the hamlet of Ap Nam O, the rice paddies, and Ap Trung Son. It was so steaming hot that the men were soaked with sweat and looked visibly drained. We waded several streams, played with leeches in the muddy ditches and paddies, and held our breaths as we treaded softly past the solemn glare of nervous water buffalo. I went along mostly as an observer to see how the squad handled it and was favorably impressed with their techniques. They kept spread out, the point and security moved well, and when a halt was called, the men would automatically turn outward for security. Finally, when we stopped to rest, the men immediately went into a perimeter defense while the squad leader supervised the men to be sure they took off their boots and wrung out their socks.

I enjoyed walking through the villages. All the children would crowd the trail and give us the thumbs-up sign, shrieking "Hello" in high-pitched voices. Some of the bolder ones would come out and grasp our hands while the more bashful hung back and stared wide-eyed at the big strangers with hair on their arms. I carried Kool-Aid and passed it out when we stopped to put mercurochrome and ointment on the ever-present scaly, festering sores that the children had on their arms and legs. Hearing the ducks and chickens underfoot and the noises of little people with their mothers calling them seemed refreshingly unreal.

One incident marred the patrol. Positioned behind me in the patrol was

Ap Nam O Village, with rice paddies in the background.

an eighteen-year-old boy from Chicago, Private R. J. Gatz, who had a loud mouth but otherwise was a pleasant-enough type. We were almost back in our perimeter and were passing through a last village and the small front yard of a South Vietnamese soldier's home when I noticed a small wicker basket filled with water and baby ducks. The next thing I realized there was uproar as the South Vietnamese soldier began yelling and waving his arms and the mother was calling her children to her and looking like she had just seen Attila the Hun. A small boy pointed to the Marine behind me. With a sheepish grin on his face, Gatz was trying to hide a little duck behind his back, hoping he would not be noticed. It was actually comical, but I immediately yelled at the man, ordered him to return the misplaced duck, and chewed him out. Sending him to the head of the column, I hoped that my immediate reaction would soothe the people. I wrote the man up when we reached base, but first I blasted him for trying to sabotage our war effort by putting a government soldier in the awkward situation in front of his wife and family of being looted by an ally. I asked him why in the hell he thought we were protecting the people from the VC if we ourselves stole from them. All this uproar occurred because a knuckleheaded kid wanted to take a duck.

Last night I went with one of our trucks and a detachment of Marines to carry a load of seven to ten Vietnamese civilians into Da Nang to one of the Vietnamese civilian hospitals. There had been a terrorist incident in the Hoa Phat hamlet marketplace. Two hand grenades had been thrown, killing a woman and a little boy and making a mess of four other women (one pregnant), several men, and some children. I took a truck over to the children's hospital at FLC, where we put the people on stretchers and in the back of the truck. Blood was all over the floor, but the Navy doctor had already given preliminary treatment, and plasma bottles were draining into the veins of those critically hurt. What astonished me were how quiet the people were and how they did not complain.

I posted security on the truck, the men locked and loaded their weapons, and we barreled down the long, deserted highway toward Da Nang. Because of the incident, I expected at least some sniper rounds to be fired at us, but we rushed past darkened houses, quiet villages squatting in the late summer heat of the curfew, and rice paddies with lush vegetation, all without a single voice or shot ringing out. As we approached the outskirts of the city, I began to make out dim shapes of people moving in the shadows of the buildings and saw the blurred images of people huddled around candlelit wooden tables, framed as they were through their open doorways. We ran into several roadblocks manned by South Vietnamese Rangers, but each time that the nervous South Vietnamese approached us with weapons held at the ready, we were waved through by the quick talking of a Vietnamese Ranger doctor who was accompanying the patients to the hospital. Finally, we wove our way through damp, garbage-littered, and abandoned streets to a hospital, where the stench of antiseptics and perspiration choked the nostrils. We stopped in the back at the emergency entrance and off-loaded the wounded civilians while excited Vietnamese bustled around, taking the victims to obscure wards. I picked up one woman who had a shrapnel-riddled leg and carried her into the hospital. It was amazing how light she was, and not once did she complain except to grimace and moan softly. Inside the hospital, people were overflowing into the halls and passageways. Every bed was dirty and contained at least two people. Apparently entire families would move in and live in the hospital or the adjacent grounds. Families had their kerosene lamps and were cooking in the rooms with kerosene stoves.

Later, after shaking hands with several South Vietnamese soldiers and medical personnel, we retraced our path to FLC. On returning to the COC, I found out more facts about the terrorist incident. An ARVN soldier was drunk and had been losing at cards that night, so he had pulled the pins on two fragmentation grenades and tossed them into the crowded marketplace.

We picked up a new lawyer for the office today. Jack Provine, from Texas, is another red-headed boy (as I am) and was a classmate at the University of Texas Law School. It is always good to see someone from home again. Bob Wachsmuth, the other classmate from the law school, just rotated home after doing a fine job here.

I finished my first company inspection. The men were drawn up by platoons for Lieutenant Colonel J. G. McCormick to inspect before he returned home. I led him through the ranks, where he had the opportunity to commend different individuals who have done an outstanding job. He later addressed the troops and said all the right things, that is, that the camp slept well knowing these men were out splashing around in the paddies, that their sacrifices were appreciated, and that he would expect to hear only good things about them in the future. All of this is certainly true about their sacrifices, but it is a shame this is the first time the command has seemed to notice it. Oh well, everyone loves a parade; the kicker is that when Joe Shit the Ragman, your average enlisted man, goes to a parade, he is it.

Later, at lunch, my friends from the legal office were kidding me about keeping the people in formation in the broiling sun for so long. Dennis Sims, with his normal pixie look of innocence, said: "Well golly, I heard a few of them say, 'It's the red-haired one we want,' and they muttered something about 'grenades' and 'we'll fix him!'" Then Dennis winked and laughed, "Of course, I didn't know what they were talking about; what do you make of it, Don?"

19 September 1968

Last night I was going to bed when I heard the stutter of automatic weapons in the paddies beyond our perimeter. I ran to the door and saw a green flare cluster go up and then heard the sucking explosions of M-79 rounds. One of our patrols had made contact. I threw on my clothes and sprinted over to the COC, where the watch officer filled me in, and I immediately made contact with the patrol by radio. They were moving across an open area and had just reached the tree line where they were to set up their ambush when they came under small-arms fire. They returned fire. I told the squad leader to be aggressive and go after the VC (easily said from the safety of the COC bunker) and not to wait for the enemy to escape. When the men reached the opposite tree line where the snipers had been, the VC had disappeared. This morning's intelligence indicates that the VC were setting in to hit us with mortars and that our patrol upset their plans, causing them to withdraw from the area.

23 September 1968

Two nights ago I went on my first night ambush patrol. It went fairly well, but it was hell to patrol the rice paddies and broken terrain in the dark. We tried to walk on the paddy dikes, but they had been weakened or washed out by the recent rains and were so narrow that we were constantly falling in the knee-high muck of the paddies. In fact, we made our best progress by wading along in the river and taking our chances with the leeches.

Coordination was a constant problem, and every time a flare popped in our vicinity, we had to throw ourselves to the ground to avoid being seen. These delays took more time. Nevertheless, there was something about taking a patrol through the different villages at night that reminded me of playing hide-and-seek as a boy. We would come softly padding into the villages and have the weird sensation of being the only ones in the village on the main paths while we could hear families eating their meals and talking inside their homes. The people do not travel at night outside their huts because it violates the curfew and puts them at risk of being shot as VC. As we paused and went into crouched positions, it was comfortable to listen to the wind sighing through the trees and to hear mothers talking to their children.

We cleared the last set of villages and were far out in the wooded islands and rice paddies. Prior to setting in our ambush on the outskirts of the village of Ap Trung Son, the sky turned yellow and lit up like a giant flickering candle. I turned and saw the flash of an explosion and then more flames from the Esso refinery, which is located five miles away on the side of a mountain and on the opposite side of the Song Cu De River. The facility, a frequent target for the VC, is guarded by Marines from First Battalion, Twenty-sixth Marine Regiment. I had our radio operator report the damage, and then, with distant flames reflecting off the sweat of the men, we moved on to our ambush site.

It took us almost six hours to cover three miles through flooded rice paddies to reach our objective. I left the patrol at an assembly area close to the village and took two point men in to scout the area. I found a good location for the machine gun and flank security, left the point men to secure the site, and went back to lead the patrol to its positions. All went uneventfully, although the men made too much noise as they took their places, and then there was the gut-wrenching effort of trying to stay awake and alert as the time dragged by. It was a losing battle. I periodically checked my men; most were exhausted and nodding off, and I would prod them awake again.

At 4:00 AM rain began to fall, which woke me up somewhat and helped keep me going as the time inched by until we could break our position and return to camp. Finally, at 5:00 AM, I gave the order to reassemble for the trip back. Almost all the patrol was in when my two right-flank security men came running back, pausing to fire their M-16s on full automatic behind them. We hit the deck. It happened in a split second, with the muzzle flashes of the weapons illuminating the jungle like strobe lights; the noise was deafening. The flank security said they had heard noises all night inching up closer to them through the jungle, and finally, when they thought they heard the sound of someone locking and loading his weapon on them, they stood up and sprayed the area and beat it back to the rest of us. The kids were shaken up, and although I do not know whether the security men actually heard anything or not, I imagine they scared the hell out of everyone in the village. I immediately took a fire team and my radio operator into the village to search it. In the process, my fire team became separated from me, and I looked back to the reassuring sight of only my radioman, who was creeping along behind me with his drawn pistol. We found nothing and linked up with the rest of the patrol on the outskirts of the village. By 7:00 AM, we had trudged back into camp, tired, with thick black smoke still billowing and smearing the sky from the Esso refinery.

I went straight to bed that morning for nearly four hours and felt like death warmed over the rest of the day. Though I piled into bed early that evening, my sleep was shattered by the alarm siren twice that night. The first time, the Army compound across the road took fifty mortar rounds, and, later, rockets hit the air base and a hospital in Da Nang. Another night was shot.

Then, last night, just before I sat down to supper, the COC paged me and told me to report to Major McMullens at First Marine Division's headquarters for a special briefing. Wearily, I had someone truck me over to the command post for the Northern Sector Defense Command, where I was briefed on a drill that was to take place that night. The planned drill was to coincide with an actual flap going on in the Da Nang area. First Marine Division was so concerned that it had disengaged one of its battalions that was fighting south of Da Nang and pulled it back into the city area for possible deployment.

I called ahead and alerted the company and formulated a scheme of maneuver on the way back to FLC. On arriving, I went straight into the COC, wrote out the order, briefed the platoon commanders, inspected the troops in the now-pouring rain, and loaded them on the trucks. Off we roared into the night on another grand adventure. I must admit that the opportunity to work with the troops in the field stirs my blood. The company's destination was Loc Hoa, where we were to block the penetration of an understrength battalion of enemy that was attempting to slip into the Da Nang environs. I planned to put a platoon on either side of the pass with one as a blocking and counterattacking force to the rear of the pass. The rain was falling in torrents, and two Marines came to guide us into the pass. Sliding and falling, the troops finally clawed their way up a muddy slope into position, and I, in turn, crawled around checking on them. At 11:00 PM, I called in artillery and illumination to the front of our position and briefed a colonel and major who came out to inspect our efforts. When the exercise was finished, the men slid back down the mountain to their trucks. There was one last snafu before we secured. A sergeant and a corporal from Third Platoon were missing when the platoons held muster, and we had to send a fire team back to find them. We waited another forty-five minutes in the rain until the missing men were found, asleep, and brought down to us. We then packed up and called it a day.

24 September 1968

A brief note of explanation—my journal dwells more on my experiences on patrols and the rifle company and rarely goes into detail concerning my daily law work or the comradeship of my friends in the office. Actually, 80 per-

Provisional Rifle Company moving into a blocking position above Loc Hoa Pass.

With the rifle company on the ridges above Loc Hoa.

cent of my time is taken up as a lawyer, but much of it is so routine in nature that my infantry duties stand out as the unusual. To this extent, my journal is out of perspective. In addition, I am grateful for my legal duties and the opportunity to work in such an interesting environment. I might not be so enchanted with infantry events if I had to deal with them all the time. In reality, much of the "grunt" routine is humdrum repetition.

Machine-gun squad moving into position above Loc Hoa Pass.

30 September 1968

Two nights ago, the VC in large numbers, a company or more, tried to take and destroy a bridge about four miles north of us. The radio reported ten VC dead almost immediately, and ground contact continued for another three hours as gunships plastered the avenues of retreat with rocket and machine-gun fire. It was like watching a science fiction movie to see the twinkling lights of the circling helicopters darting about in the sky, followed by long pencil streaks of brilliant red from the Gatling guns. When the gunships unleashed their rockets, instantaneous flashes mushroomed across the valley floor, followed seconds later by the quick thumps of explosions. I learned later that one Marine on the bridge had been hit in the head by enemy fire and would probably die.

We are reporting increased contact all through our immediate area. Seabee construction crews working on our new perimeter have been sniped at. We send out patrols now to protect them. A large patrol went out last night and had a small group of six slide off from the main body as a stay-behind ambush. They are to be there two days and two nights. Last night, they spotted seven VC moving on an adjoining island and went after them with hand grenades, M-79 rounds, and small-arms fire. They had a running firefight and at first light found evidence of fresh blood.

Last night I lost myself in the beautiful story of *Gigi* on a projection screen set up in the chow hall. I had never seen the movie before, and the chance to lose myself in the boulevards of Paris at the turn of the century was delightful. When I walked outside after the movie was over, the same area was again lit by flares, and tracers stitched silent patterns across the distant hills. There is so much living to be done, and I feel deep pity and sadness for anyone who dies in this far-off war over people and issues about which the bulk of America seems to know so little.

2 October 1968

I have just been assigned my first murder case to defend. The lad, Private First Class Roman Serrano, hails from Cincinnati. He is twenty-two or twenty-three years old, tall, and fairly muscular, with oddly set eyes that seem to glow with yellow sulfur. He is charged with felony murder. It looks as if he killed a man with a piece of lead pipe and robbed him; then he attacked and tried to do a job on another individual. He has a long record of violent crimes, and I am sure he needs psychiatric evaluation. Of course, I may have gained a poor impression of this individual due to the circumstances of our first meeting. He was in maximum security at the brig and locked in an enclosed square metal box, where he was left to cook in the heat.

8 October 1968

Last week we were entertained with a USO show by a group of Filipinos with two luscious female singers, a backup band, and an aging American comedian who has made the circuit several times but who was still very entertaining. All of us from the legal shop crowded around a table to the side of the platform that served as a stage when we got the word that General Olson and his staff would be unable to attend the performance because they had guests to entertain at headquarters. Like a greased flash, the junior officers moved in and took the prime seats with the Griff placing himself directly in front of and two feet from the stage. When the first little singer came out, I turned a deep red, blushing from pure happiness and delight. She had a perfect body and a cute face, was very talented in her singing, and twisted it out in little gyrating Do moves. We looked deep into each other's eyes throughout her routine, and I know that she only had eyes for me. Later she came back in a short minidress, and I jumped onto the stage to dance with her. The other girl wore a low-cut dress and kept saying to the slobbering, whistling, foot-stomping audience, "I love you!" By this time, the American comedian who ran the show was in the bag from all the drinks pressed on him, and we managed to get the girls into the bar, where we toasted their beauty. They happily agreed with us.

I have been interviewing witnesses in the Serrano case and am coming up with the picture of an extremely strange man. This tall, muscular individual with a catlike walk wears his fatigue cap crushed down like a touring cap. He comes from the slums of Cincinnati, had a broken home, hates most symbols of authority or restraint, and resents people who come from happier and more secure backgrounds. Although white, he actively dislikes white people, and nearly everyone he can call a friend is black. He preaches Black Power to all the black Marines around him and builds up a following by giving free Cokes to them and keeping a complete collection of soul music to attract the men into his hut. He tells his black friends that he is a gypsy and has more to hate the "honkies" for than black people do because the whites have annihilated the gypsies. Yet, he uses the black Marines. He never lets them consider him as just one of them. He has to be the leader and assumes a superior air in telling them how to handle their racial problems. He apparently likes to have the black Marines around and to have them look up to him because it flatters his ego. Yet, he cheats them in cards when he plays. He goes into violent fits and becomes involved in fights defending black people against real or imagined slights when he is not even involved in the discussion. He is an excellent and hard worker when assigned a difficult job but is a poor worker when given routine tasks. He is intelligent but is only impressed by strong, decisive people and is contemptuous of weak, indecisive people. He has a fetish for keeping clean hands; he will wash his hands before lighting a cigarette. He has a long history of aggressive violence, but his habit is to pick up a club or pipe rather than to use his hands. He has nearly everyone terrified of him at his base, yet it is interesting to note that his black friends are the most afraid of him. Another quirk about this man is that, when talking to an officer or NCO, he will talk in a Cincinnati street accent, but when talking to black people he switches to an Alabaman-type, deep Southern accent.

I hope I can accumulate enough information on him to have him declared criminally insane; otherwise, he faces the real likelihood of life imprisonment. (Serrano subsequently requested that his defense be handled by Chuck Cherry, who had represented him on a prior charge. He was tried and convicted on part of the charges alleged against him.)

9 / Night Assault

13 October 1968

I have just finished an intense experience. Last night I took the company into the village of Ap Trung Son in what I believe to be the first night helicopter assault in our area of operation. I know it was my first.

It all began when I received an intelligence report that indicated there was a high probability that FLC would be attacked by mortars from Ap Trung Son on one of the nights of October 11, 12, or 13. It occurred to me that the Army Air Calvary had a repair unit down the road and that maybe I could talk them into making some helicopters available for a night assault. Amazingly, my plan was approved at FLC. Arbitrarily picking the night of October 12 as the attack date, I went over to the Air Calvary repair unit, where I talked to the colonel and his executive officer, a lieutenant colonel. What they had available were either helicopters that had been shot up or wrecked helicopters that they were trying to patch back together. When I asked for their help, they could not have been more eager to cooperate. In fact, the colonel flew the lead helicopter.

The rifle platoon that was picked for the assault was briefed earlier in the day, and we left FLC on trucks at mid-afternoon, hoping that no one would notice our going to the Army compound. That night we ate dinner in the Army mess hall, and then we went out onto the helicopter pads for equipment inspections and to wait until it was time to go. After all of the last-minute checks were completed, I walked around talking with the men and noted that they were unusually quiet, with nervous conversations going on in small groups.

Approaching one of our Navy corpsmen who was in deep discussion with several Marines, I overheard them speaking about what to do with enemy wounded in the event a firefight left both injured Marines and Viet Cong. The Marines were of the opinion that it was not their responsibility, or the corpsman's, to care for the enemy wounded. The corpsman felt otherwise and asked my opinion. I told him that his first responsibility was to take care of any wounded Marines but that we were not animals and that the enemy should receive the same treatment as our own, if possible. Besides, a living VC had intelligence value, and a dead one did not.

We were scheduled to lift off at precisely 1:00 AM, and, at that moment, the rain clouds parted, revealing a beautiful full moon as the choppers rose into the night sky. The men were packed inside the Hueys, and the leaders' legs dangled out the doors so they could be first out. With the familiar beating noise of rotors, the lead helicopter turned toward the South China Sea to gain height and then made a wide swing back inland toward Ap Trung Son. Through patches of clouds, bright silvery moonlight reflected off the rain-saturated rice paddies below, interspersed with dark areas of shadowy, sleeping hamlets. The helicopters then descended quickly and came in low to the ground to a sandy area behind Ap Trung Son on which a graveyard was situated. They slowed momentarily as Marines dropped to the ground, assembled, and then moved off in the darkness into the village.

We began to have sightings of the enemy almost immediately, and sporadic fire soon broke out. As squads dispersed through the village along narrow trails, they soon encountered scattered resistance. By 4:30 AM we were headed home with five VC to our credit. By a stroke of luck, one of the enemy prisoners was the VC district chief. He was shot in a running firefight, dragged to a small clearing on the edge of the village, and subsequently medivaced in a Huey gunship. He is going to live, after extensive surgery, and I am informed that he has provided valuable intelligence about the VC forces in our area.

These were exhilarating moments. The men had been drilled and briefed countless times, and when I landed with my radio operator in the second assault wave, I saw crouched Marines running to assemble where their squad leaders were set up and then move to their preassigned objectives. One platoon moved into blocking positions to the north of the village while another helilifted in. I kept Third Platoon in reserve at the helipad in case it was needed. The only casualties were eight people from the blocking platoon who triggered a land mine. Fortunately, none were hurt seriously.

Two squads encircled the village while a third squad swept through it, moving through backyards and down narrow village paths lined with tall cane. I was walking down one path when troops fired at two figures running away at a trail intersection, but we did not follow them because I was in a hurry to push through to the far end of the village, where I could call in mortar fire on the surrounding paddy areas to prevent anyone's escape. In the dark, as the rifle fire erupted around us, we could not tell who was shooting at whom, and the situation reminded me how General Stonewall Jackson had been shot by mistake by his own men in the deepening darkness and confusion at the end of the day at the Battle of Chancellorsville.

An artilleryman would have been horrified at the slapdash manner we had of calling in fire. I gave the mortar crews standing by at FLC a rough azimuth to the map coordinates for prearranged targets in and around the village, but I could not see where the rounds were landing. I would call for mortar fire on a given target, receive a "shot out" back over the radio to let us know that the round was on the way, and then everyone would scramble for a ditch and work up high hopes that the round did not land on top of us. Then, there would be a ground-shaking "kawoomp" somewhere nearby. I would count noses and then call in another set of coordinates, hoping that my map reading was accurate. By this time, I was separated from the rest of the men who were throughout the village, and my concern now was that our own people would be shooting at each other and that the mortar fire could hit our own troops. To check where the high explosives were landing, I called for illumination rounds. The illumination rounds were duly fired, and, making a soft whistling sound, the parachute flares lazily floated down directly over the center of the village. I called a cease-fire. Later I was relieved to learn that the illumination rounds had been short and that the high-explosive rounds had not been landing in the middle of Ap Trung Son as a part of my urban renewal efforts.

I gradually worked my way to the troops that had swept through the village by having them pop hand illumination flares and discovered a wounded VC, wearing a tan uniform, moaning on the ground. He had walked up to the platoon commander and another Marine, apparently thinking they were part of his men, and given them an order. The Marine lance corporal replied with his own order, "Dung Lai!" (Halt!) and then shot him as he tried to escape. The Marine and his platoon commander followed the wounded VC into a hut, where he threw out a Chicom grenade, but its blast missed them. They pulled him out of the hut, and he was on a poncho by the path when I came up. We moved him to the closest clearing and, after calling in a medivac chopper, went through the items he was carrying in a waterproof bag. He had a diary with a picture of a nude American girl, official documents, several bottles of Russian pills, a canteen (U.S.), 782 gear (canvas map case and ammo belts), a Chinese 9 mm automatic pistol, passes of some sort, rice, letters, and a bag of salt. I turned the documents over to intelligence but made sure that the pistol was tagged and locked away so that the lance corporal who captured it could later take it home with him.

When I came upon the wounded Viet Cong, he lay moaning in pain after having been shot point blank in the abdomen by an M-16. His uniform was soaked in blood as the corpsman who had questioned earlier what to do with a wounded enemy worked feverishly to stop the bleeding. Standing behind the corpsman and leaning over the Vietnamese was also one of the Marines whom I had talked to earlier; he kept repeating to the injured man in a calm tone that he was going to be all right.

I was so enthusiastic about what the company had accomplished that on the way home to base I took the point and promptly led everyone into rice paddies that ran from six inches to five feet deep. We literally had to swim home at times, but no one cared.

10 / Racial Tensions Boil Over

17 October 1968

Private Jerome James from Maintenance Battalion went to trial the day after our night helicopter assault on Ap Trung Son. James was accused of being involved in a racial beating and attempted murder at the heavy-equipment recreation room last July. The facts reflected that he and two other black Marines went by the heavy-equipment club the night before the incident and were apparently invited in to have a drink by a drunk white boy. Once they were inside they were told they would have to leave because the club was off-limits to all but heavy-equipment personnel, whether red, black, white, or yellow. This angered the black Marines, and an argument followed, with James apparently going off with his friends into the dark of the night, muttering threats. James apparently then went to search for some fellow black Marines to help them take on the whites who had told them to leave, but none were willing to become involved. The following night, however, a group of black Marines assembled and returned to the club, breaking through the door and working the occupants over with knives, hammers, chains, fists, and assorted playthings. This mayhem rattled James, and he then went to the Criminal Investigative Department, where he reported that he was present and could say who perpetrated the crime. He was charged with being an accomplice.

James gave such a convincing story of confusion and misidentification in this brawl that I believed his innocence. Unfortunately, he kept getting into trouble for new offenses, and more and more charges were piled on for me to defend. His chances of seeing daylight became more and more remote. James's friends had attacks of amnesia and were not willing to testify who they did see commit the offenses instead of James. Instead, they have fabricated a little dog-and-pony-show to give him an alibi, placing him at the scene only as an innocent onlooker.

While his case was pending, the kid went absent without leave twice, misappropriated a vehicle, violated bunches of orders, and did all that could be done to ruin himself. There was only one ray of hope: he thought I was a swell lawyer.

I went by to talk to his colonel about dropping some of the minor charges against him and was politely asked if I would like to talk to my client first. They brought him in at 1:30 PM completely intoxicated. My pleas for mercy fell on deaf ears.

James's trial ran for three days and involved many issues of law concerning confessions and eyewitness identifications. My main defense was that of mistaken identity because the two eyewitnesses had only a few moments to observe him. Their fleeting observations also took place during the confusion of a fight in the tight confines of a small room when some eight black individuals suddenly appeared, swinging lethal weapons. Three witnesses identified another black Marine as the first person through the door, whereas two identified James; of the two who identified James, however, one had identified another person at the lineup and said that he was James, and the other gave a physical description after the melee that did not fit James. Both of them only identified James for the first time at the pretrial investigation, which occurred some six weeks after the original crime. This identification took place under highly suggestive circumstances, with all the white witnesses seated together talking freely across from the two accused black individuals. The trial was a very long and emotional one because it involved a heinous crime where many people were stabbed, beaten, and knocked senseless. James also had additional charges—twice being in off-limits areas after curfew, which violated orders. James pled guilty to one off-limits charge but was able to have a motion for finding of not guilty granted on the other charge when the government forgot to introduce evidence on it. All in all, I think having several enlisted members, including three black sergeants, on the court helped immensely. After many hours, the court acquitted James of all the assault charges. He had pled guilty, however, to being in an off-limits area and was found guilty on a charge of wrongful appropriation of a government vehicle. Although there was not enough evidence to convict him, I was afraid that the court would use these charges as an indirect means to punish James for the assaults. So, prior to sentencing, I had him take the stand, where I questioned him about his involvement in the assaults on which he had been acquitted. The court snapped to attention. Courts usually wonder whether they have acquitted a guilty person, and now they could find out. James testified he was not involved in the actual crime but that he was a witness, knew who had been the perpetrators, and would testify in coming trials to ensure that the real criminals were punished. The court gave him only two months' confinement. This climaxed a fast-moving, glorious week.

11 / Trials under Fire, a Trip to the *Repose*, and the Marine Corps Birthday

29 October 1968

Several days after the James case, I went on another night ambush patrol. We left from an artillery battery about a mile from FLC and hugged the villages along the rain-swollen, leech-infested rice paddies, hoping to creep craftily into Ap Trung Son to set up the ambush. We were less than silent, however. The damned ducks and dogs of the Vietnamese we were passing honked and quacked and howled like a zoo. It was like bringing Dr. Doolittle's circus to town. We finally cleared the villages along the paddies and slipped and oozed into Ap Trung Son. Part of our frustration was the fact that Twenty-sixth Marines across the river were in heavy contact, and their illumination flares made us stand out like statues as we moved in the open. Time and again we had to freeze and drop to the ground. We would go a few more feet, another flare would go up, and we would freeze again. This nerve-wracking exercise went on for more than an hour. Then, the last two men in the rear of the patrol got lost, and we had to go back and find them.

Between 11:30 PM and 1:00 AM we moved into our ambush site. Instead of setting up on the outskirts of the village, we moved into the center, set up at a crossroad of paths, and established a killing zone that would clear out anyone who came from any direction. Then we waited. And we waited. It began to rain, and a chill that penetrated to the bone crept in. My eyes felt like they had been stabbed with pins; my head ached; and the time crawled by. At 5:30 AM we pulled in our security and quietly filed out of the slumbering village. No contact. Whether we had been seen and the VC notified or whether the VC simply were not there, I will never know. We made the long trek back to base, wading through the paddies and skirting hamlets in the early dawn. Finally, we topped out on the sand flats for the last one-half to one mile back to camp. I was extremely pleased with how the patrol performed. As we emerged onto the open sand, the squad professionally fell into staggered formation, spread out, and sent out flank and rear security.

The following day the Communists made their presence known again. At noon, one of the daylight patrols was crossing an island in our area when a booby trap went off that mangled the foot of one Marine and blasted shrapnel into the face and body of the man behind him. The patrol moved in a 360° sweep to search for other mines. A Marine stepped on another one, but it did not go off. We called the Army for a medivac helicopter, and the Army pilots responded promptly to get our wounded out of the rice paddies and on the way to skilled care. The morale of the rest of the platoon has been affected, however, since this incident.

2 November 1968

The Marine who stepped on the booby trap was taken to the hospital ship *Repose*, which was anchored off Phu Bai. Navy doctors were unable to save his foot, and it had to be amputated. I subsequently caught a flight out of Da Nang to Phu Bai and went aboard the ship to see how he was doing.

The *Repose* is a large hospital ship, painted white, with large red crosses on its sides and a helicopter landing deck. It is equipped with the latest medical technology. Doctors and nurses provide skilled care equal to the best anywhere. With luck, a wounded Marine may be carried by helicopter in a matter of minutes from a rice paddy to the *Repose*, where his chances of survival increase dramatically.

The different decks contained different wards and surgical suites. Those less severely injured rested in their blue pajamas on their racks or played cards. Some lay quietly, enduring their pain. The most severely injured were transferred to Japan and then back to the States.

I found my corporal, and he appeared to be pleased, and embarrassed, to be visited by an officer. He gave me some messages to pass on to his friends at FLC and talked about going back to college. I thanked him for his service, and we visited until a nurse came in to treat him. He never complained.

6 November 1968

I have just finished defending Private Mike Blannik in a case that ran for four days at First Military Police Battalion. He was accused of striking a superior NCO (a corporal) and of being disrespectful. I brought in evidence that put the corporal on trial rather than Blannik. I did not want to sit quietly on the defensive because the law is particularly dangerous for a private when he is accused of striking a noncommissioned officer. I discredited the corporal by showing that he was shacking up with a Vietnamese girl out in the village and giving her government food from the mess hall. Then, when my man threatened to report him, the corporal shoved him, and Blannik punched him out. There were also instances of the corporal's trying to have others perjure themselves on the stand and to say they saw Blannik hit the corporal first. He also threatened others not to testify on the stand on Blannik's behalf. The facts made Corporal Jeff Dunn sound like an ogre and Blannik like a saint, but both are yardbirds in some respects, with redeeming traits; they are just men. The verdict was for the defense.

The day before yesterday I flew to Dong Ha to try Sergeant Richard Ryan's case for assault with a dangerous weapon on a superior officer and for assault and battery on a lance corporal. Because Dong Ha has taken some heavy-artillery incoming fire for the last few days, everyone is on edge. The compound of FLSG-B is zeroed in on and gets hit with sickening regularity. Several nights ago, Hanoi Hanna broadcast that NVA troops would eat in our mess hall within the next week, and two days later it was hit by direct hits from their artillery. Two nights ago, she said the officers would not have a place to enjoy drinks at night for very much longer (now she has made us mad!), so everyone has been expecting our little building where we drink our booze to be obliterated.

Two days before I arrived in Dong Ha, FLSG-B had taken forty-two rounds of artillery one afternoon and more than sixty the next day. We took several rounds the afternoon I arrived, which were just enough to keep everyone gun-shy. That first day, I prepared my case, lined up witnesses, and talked to Sergeant Ryan. He is a big, rugged man with a moustache, a pockmarked face, and a sixteen-year career in the Corps. Still, he is only a buck sergeant after all this time. He hit a lance corporal and pulled a pistol on a warrant officer but claimed to be under a mental blackout at the time. Actually, he has a past mental record of depressive blackouts and at the time was under a family strain with his Panamanian wife and child, his work, and threats on his life by some of his troops. I had psychiatric tests run on him, which stated he was sane but a nut, and I argued mental incapacity at the time of the offense, which resulted in an acquittal. The good, crazy sergeant is free, but I would not want him to move next door to me in the neighborhood.

The world news is picking up. There is a bombing halt, which was obviously called for political reasons because it came so close to the elections, and then Richard Nixon has managed to squeak into the White House. In the meantime, two young Marines lost their legs due to booby traps while on patrol. The whole area is a festering sore of mines and booby traps. We retaliate with artillery and mortar fire in the areas where the VC set their mines. They generally set them up on the islands in our tactical area. Last night we fired mortar rounds at an island that seems to be constantly booby-trapped and later found that one round made a direct hit on an unlucky VC.

The old-timers are rotating out of the office now. Only Dennis Sims of the old crew is left, but he goes home at the end of this month. Jerry Cunningham and Jim Haydel have both returned to other lives. At the same time, new officers have come on board as replacements, bringing their own unique talents. I have not previously mentioned Charlie Babcock, a talented musician who sang in college productions of Broadway musicals. On quiet evenings, while others pass time playing cards, we hear Charlie's clear voice singing operatic arias from his Quonset hut office or listen to him playing the piano in the bar.

Halloween, which is also my mom and dad's anniversary, has come and gone again. I appropriately dressed in green like a big dill pickle this year. The next holiday is the Marine Corps' birthday this coming Sunday. A lot of time and space is behind me since this time last year when I was a lieutenant at The Basic School at Quantico, Virginia, and when I had one of the finest weekends of my life; the autumn leaves of Virginia, a beautiful date, the dress ball, and good friends are only happy memories now.

10 November 1968

Today is the United States Marine Corps' 193rd birthday—193 years of faithful service as one of the finest fighting organizations the world has ever known. Even though we are in a war zone, we celebrated our birthday last night and cheered the passing of another year for the Corps. Our ceremony was a traditional one, in which the honor guard posted the colors and then General Olson marched up to the speakers' platform and thanked the men for their service. Next, the officer of the day read a birthday message from the commandant, with each part of the ceremony interspersed with bugle calls. The highlight of the ceremony involved a huge cake that the cooks had somehow concocted and had carried into the middle of the mess hall. The general took a dress sword and sliced the first two pieces. The first piece always goes to the oldest Marine, and the second piece goes to youngest Marine.

Of course, there was a tremendous meal of steak (water buffalo, I think) with all the trimmings that a man dreams about, and the Seabees from across the road were generous enough to send over an outstanding band to serenade us. It was a fine night. My platoon commanders kept pouring beer on me, while I bought them drinks. When the band broke into a polka, big Gene Schwartzlow, who runs Second Platoon, strutted out on the floor and did a bouncing, nimble polka while everyone clapped and cheered. These are good men.

12 / A Difficult Client

In late August 1968, the luck of the draw presented me with another Seabee to defend. He was a pathetic worm named Petty Officer Sam Preston. It was not that I disliked him. I simply had no reason to warm up to his personality, his deeds, or his words. He ran down and killed a Vietnamese National Police officer while in his weapons carrier in what apparently was honestly an accident, although he is charged with negligent homicide. Preston was passing a row of trucks when one pulled out without looking behind and forced him into a ditch, where he met an ARVN policeman coming toward him on a motorcycle. After the collision, Preston backed up and ran for it, leaving the cycle looking like a broken junk pile and the Vietnamese policeman spread along the barbed wire fence. I honestly believe that if he would have stayed and not panicked that he would not be in trouble, but when he ran away he nearly ran over a Marine major, who proceeded to chase him down by jeep.

Waiting in a war zone while the gears of military justice ground slowly ahead was unnerving to Preston. Another delay occurred when the Marine major went on temporary leave. While the rest of his Seabee battalion rotated home, Preston lingered. As the prosecution had a paint analysis performed on the vehicles and prepared witnesses for the article 32 investigation, Preston used his time to write his congressman to complain that he had incompetent counsel and had not been sent home yet. He was a worrier and would come and sit in my office, where he would question and worry for hours. I tolerated him only because I felt sorry for him and his misery. But I did not like his attitude, which showed no regret for killing a Vietnamese, except to the extent that it inconvenienced him with these charges.

When the article 32 was run, I was pleasantly surprised. The Navy lawyer did a rush job on setting up the investigation, scheduling it for 8:00 AM on a Wednesday, but the first notice I received was not until 6:30 AM Wednesday morning. I did not show. The major and everyone else did, with the major walking out in a rage, slamming the door and making very threatening statements against Preston. The next day I prepared to approach a screeching, slobbering wildcat, but just the opposite happened. When the major entered the room and saw that I was a Marine officer, he immediately became cordial, pleasant, and even helpful. He made statement after statement that helped us, such as "It looked to me like he had plenty of room when he started to pass," "I imagine he thought there was enough room," and so on. The government counsel looked dumbfounded and did not even offer a rebuttal argument. I had hopes that Preston would only have to go to trial for fleeing the scene of an accident and not for negligent homicide—but no such luck.

Preston's general court-martial started on a Sunday morning. It was a two-day case on charges of fleeing the scene of the accident (to which he pled guilty), involuntary manslaughter, and reckless driving. The first day was generally a disaster, and I spent it in a rear-guard action of cross-examination of one of their key witnesses that got absolutely nowhere. The only break was that the prosecution called many Vietnamese witnesses who had conflicting and confusing stories. The Vietnamese are a good people, but when put in an American court run by American rules, unique problems can arise. The trial counsel had some initial problems with administering the oath but eventually came up with "Do you swear that the evidence you are about to give in the case now in hearing to be the truth, the whole truth, and nothing but the truth, so help you Buddha?"

That night I believed our case was going badly and that much of it was probably my fault. I had been tired all day, handled my questioning amateurishly, and generally was just dissatisfied with it all. We recessed at 9:00 PM, and I went back to Red Beach for a few hours of sleep before getting up early the next morning and going at it again.

I felt more rested the next day, however, and the arguments went more smoothly. I hammered on the inconsistencies in the government's case and emphasized the reasonableness of Preston's actions. Eventually the court closed to deliberate. They deliberated for more than three hours and then came back with findings of not guilty of reckless driving and involuntary manslaughter and guilty of negligent homicide and fleeing the scene of the accident.

Then began the real battle—to come out of this scrambled situation with an acceptable sentence. I pointed out Preston's fine record in the Army and National Guard, including an honorable discharge into the Navy. I reminded the court that in his ten years of service Preston had never committed an offense. Finally, I had him describe his background and his plans for the future with his family (this caused him to break down and cry on the stand). The courtroom was charged with emotion. I then argued for no confinement under the circumstances because it would serve no useful purpose other than vengeance. The court closed and deliberated another two hours. When it reopened, it gave Preston a fine of $100.00 per month for six months and a reduction of one pay grade. There was no confinement and no bad-conduct discharge. Preston was overwhelmed with joy and blurted out, "Thank you very much, sir!"

Preston has been a stubborn, taciturn man, weak in some aspects but sincere and outspoken in others. He surprised me the next day by coming into my office and meekly knocking before poking his head in to "see if I was busy." When I told him to come in, he gave me a new leather briefcase (he had noticed that I did not have one) and a fifth of Black & White scotch. He awkwardly poked his toe around the floor and told everyone within hearing what a fine lawyer I was, shook hands, and left for the States. This was a far cry from the day he had started a congressional investigation on me.

13 / Thanksgiving and a Trip to Saigon

18 November 1968

This past week was one marked by sameness of routine: paperwork at the office, workouts, administrative work on the Provisional Rifle Company, and so on, until night before last. Once again, as the siren's wail shook us from our sleep, we were sent stumbling and crawling to the bunkers in the middle of the night. At 1:30 AM the VC hit the air base with ten rockets that were obviously fired close to FLC because several people saw the flashes as they were fired. There were no casualties. At the same time, bands of NVA infiltrators attacked traffic and police stations inside Da Nang. Lieutenant Steve Carney, a motor transport officer, was in Da Nang at the time and just barely missed an ambush where a jeep with three Vietnamese National Police officers was shot up, killing them all. At 4:30 AM the alarm screeched again, and this time another ten rockets impacted in the shore party's area and the Seabee camp. At each alarm, I scrambled into my clothes and sprinted to the COC to muster with the company and see whether we would be called out. The second trip to the bunker was more personal for my people; we learned that a seven-man patrol of First Battalion, Twenty-sixth Marines, operating within one hundred meters of the limits of our tactical area, was overrun and all of its men killed. Apparently, they had already set in their ambush site when they were overrun. I imagine they went to sleep, but it is only a guess. This is a grim warning to the men about complacency because it could have been us instead of them.

The VC have redoubled their efforts in our area recently by setting numerous booby traps. One of my patrols was led to a cache of Chicom grenades near our base three days ago. Local children told the Marines where the weapons were located, and they also told the Marines that the VC had been active recently in the nearby villages. The VC also apparently told the villagers to stay off the islands in the nearby rice paddies because they were booby-trapped. One boy said he saw a stray dog go across one island and detonate an explosive device.

Yesterday, Sunday, 17 November, I took my men to the beach area of NCB-22 (Seabees) for a day of rest. We loaded up on steaks, beer, sun, and interplatoon competition. Teams competed in volleyball, tugs-of-war, tackle football, and beer chug-a-lug contests. The laughing and cheering troops threw the platoon commanders and me into the ocean. In tackle football we banged heads with fierce abandon, helped by the fact that most were fortified by liberal amounts of the suds. It was a perfect day.

We returned to base in time to have another muster at the COC because of a new alert condition in the Da Nang area. Again last night, the VC hit our area. They fired mortars on the Army helicopter pad across the road from us about 1:30 AM. What disgusts me is the fact that the enemy mortars were operated out of the same village where a South Vietnamese PF group and a Rural Development Unit are stationed for pacification purposes. They have been there about three weeks and have another two weeks to go. Our wonderful allies reek of either rank incompetence or outright treachery. In this case, probably both are true.

In the meantime, I am being kicked upstairs here in the legal office and being transferred from the defense section to the prosecution section. I am a "cop" now, and "Dirty Jack" Provine gives me hell about it. That is the price one has to pay for respectability!

28 November 1968

Today is Thanksgiving in Vietnam, and I have been pondering my many blessings. I treasure life so much more now and want very much to live through these times. I hope that I will never again be overly concerned with the minor problems of life nor take for granted the simple luxuries we enjoy. I know that this will always be a period in my life of which I will be fiercely proud. In the meantime, I continue to dream of the Triumph sports car I intend to buy when I get home, and I downshift in my sleep.

Last Tuesday night, 19 November, Soviet-made 122 mm rockets pounded our base, but our casualties were considered light. One lieutenant was killed in his office when it took a direct hit, and we had many other less-serious wounds. At the time, I was in the COC preparing the company to go on an operation early the next morning. When I finished my preparations I lay down on a cot to get an hour's rest and read from Bernard Fall's classic history of the battle of Dien Bien Phu, *Hell in a Very Small Place*. As I was drifting off to sleep, the lights in the bunker suddenly went out, followed by a thunderclap of noise. While dust and debris poured from the ceilings, the sirens went off, and I had a brief moment of confusion as to where I was and which war was going on.

I jumped up and went out to be sure that the men were in their trenches and under cover. As the base siren was wailing its pitiful warning, large explosions were going off all around us, making huge sucking sounds, like air rushing into gigantic vacuums. Soon, someone gave the word for everyone to take cover inside the COC, and the bunker began to fill with men. Overcrowding made the COC dangerous, however, so I herded them out after making sure they had their helmets and flak jackets on. None of my people were hurt, but rocket shrapnel wounded four Marines in an adjacent tent.

At 1:00 AM we moved out and clamped a cordon around the village of Mieu Thach Son. At first light, we moved the people into an assembly area on the sand behind their houses, where they were segregated, searched, and checked against our blacklists of VC suspects. We determined seven to be VC suspects, two of whom were confirmed as VC agents who had just recently come back from a Communist school in the hills, where they were trained in bobby traps. For their final exam, they have blown the legs off two of my men; the two VC agents were two fourteen-year-old girls.

The following day I was ordered to go to Saigon with Ron Williamson (the Round Mound) to a three-day legal conference. We were up early but could not find the section of the airfield where the naval passenger plane was supposed to leave. We finally found it as the aircraft was beginning to taxi and was closing its door. I had the driver of my jeep pull alongside, and I hollered, "Is this plane going to Saigon?" When a "yes" came back, we threw

Ron Williamson on the rooftop of the Anatole Restaurant, Saigon, late November 1968.

our bags on board and climbed in. I had forgotten my orders but could not have cared less. I promptly fell asleep.

Saigon is too much to attempt to describe. It had honest-to-God traffic jams and civilians. It seemed to steam with an atmosphere of intrigue, corruption, and desperate gaiety. There seemed to be even less resolution for getting the job done than there was in the rest of the country. The legal conference served only to highlight conflicts between some of the State Department personnel in Saigon and top officials of the Military Assistance Council, Vietnam, over the direction of the war. I went only one day, and the next day Ron and I skipped out. We then spent one of the most pleasant days of the past five months. We walked the streets, taking pictures, and tried to get into the barbed-wire-ringed president's palace, where we were politely shown the door. Later we bargained for silk in the marketplace and dined like kings at various restaurants. The prices were shocking, but we swaggered into the best hotels in town in our jungle utilities and dined on fine filets and wine. At night we went to the French-styled bars on the rooftops of the hotels and relaxed over drinks while looking out over the city to the distant Mekong Delta. It made us dream of another life. Naturally, we took in the

Saigon bars and the bar girls, on whom we spent $30.00 in one and one-half hours. I found out that "Saigon tea" is a weak tea that the girls constantly order while they snuggle up to you. It costs two dollars a shot and is a subtle form of highway robbery. The girls all have tragic stories to tell, are all beautiful, and are as clever as she-wolves. The trip was a happy, three-day example of how a fool and his money are soon parted.

The most enjoyable experience took place one morning as Ron and I were walking in the area of the presidential palace. We came up on a large group of young Vietnamese schoolchildren dressed in white shirts and blue shorts or skirts. They were coming from a Catholic school and were paired off and holding hands while Catholic sisters anxiously bustled around them. We walked out and helped stop traffic for them while, wide-eyed and giggling, they crossed the street to attend Mass in a beautiful cathedral. We followed them in and sat through the service. It was a moment of beautiful peace, distancing us from the war around us. The children's voices came from another world in this ancient cathedral that slumbered in a grandeur reminiscent of medieval France. After a while we noticed that the little girls were laughing at us and that the little boys across the aisle were shyly pointing our way. Grownup men should have known better than to do something silly like sit on the girls' side of the church.

14 / War in the Christmas Season

1 December 1968

The night before last we were hit twice. Most of the rounds fell short and outside our perimeter, and the rest fell in the swamp on the Truck Company area, causing no casualties or damage. Nothing exceptional resulted this time except that crater analysis shows that the rounds are 140 mm rockets for the first time instead of 122 mm. They were equipped with delayed-action fuses that can penetrate and destroy any of our bunkers. Everyone is busy sandbagging around the hooch areas, expecting that the worst may be yet to come.

I am now chief in the trial section, and the pace is fast and grinding. The colonel wants more cases tried this month, and right now it looks like I will have seven general courts, plus the rifle company, plus a stack of papers, plus routine administrative duties to handle this month. December should go by in a blur.

5 December 1968

This period is a frantic one, to say the least. Colonel Haden is either constantly calling "Red!" or sending someone back for me, saying, "Sir, the colonel wants to see you!" The colonel is a fine, wonderful man who has the distracting habit of having the shortest memory of anyone I have ever met. He will call me in and ask what is happening in the Zell case. I will tell him, and ten minutes later when I go back in with further information he wanted, I will have to reexplain who Zell is. He is noted for calling out to the top sergeant and saying, "Top, get me Colonel Fowler on the phone!" The top then anxiously does his act and dials and fumes and finally gets through. The dialogue usually goes something like this: "Sir, Colonel Fowler is on the phone." "Colonel Fowler, what does he want? Take a message from him!" Or I can be working, trying to get out some rush material, and invariably the colonel will decide that it is the time to walk back to our offices, sit down, and engage in morale-building conversations. "Well, Red, what's going on?"

If we concentrate on it, with a minimum of effort we can keep several large crises and numerous minor ones boiling all at once. It is amusing to watch everyone go bouncing off the walls when the colonel starts his daily routine of shouting for answers to questions that we answered yesterday or demanding reports that are already on his desk. There could not be a bigger-hearted man or a finer officer, but his eccentricities leave us buggy at the end of a day.

The enemy activity in our area continues to increase. This past week, First Lieutenant James Petersen took his Third Platoon on a helicopter-borne, two-day sweep of the Mieu Na Island area that resulted in the ambush of a sixteen-man NVA/VC rice-gathering party with no loss to the Marines. They captured the rice as well as documents that showed that at least one of the enemy was an NVA private who had received a meritorious mention for his efforts against the Americans. Another letter from another NVA to this same man told him that he would pay his indebtedness as soon as he got some cash. Canned food, medicine, and clothing were picked up. The patrol found blood but no bodies. There were slide marks in the mud and discarded banana leaf compresses stuck together with fresh blood. The rice sacks were perforated with bullet holes, and the enemy packs were shredded with M-79 fragments.

The night before last I went out with a squad-sized patrol so that I could observe the performance of some of the new men. We went through Ap Trung Son in the afternoon, where we probed the haystacks for enemy arms and caches, with zero results. We then waited for dark before we moved out through the paddies to set up an ambush along the river. Just after we left the village and were about one hundred meters out in the paddy, a sniper opened up on us. When the first bullet cracked over our heads, we dropped to the ground and rolled into the muck and slime of the paddy for cover. After five shots, the firing stopped. No one was hit, but we had not seen a muzzle flash to show us where Charlie was located. We called in a report to the COC and continued our patrol.

That night it was pitch dark, and although the patrol split up twice, we were lucky that the separated groups did not shoot at one another before the patrol reunited. We walked down a river twice along the patrol route. Once the water was almost over my head, and only my hands—with my camera in one and my rifle in the other—were out of the water. Unfortunately (or maybe fortunately), we did not run into anything that night.

7 December 1968

Last night the VC mortared the adjacent Army helicopter pad. They fired off four rounds when the patrol, which was led by Corporal Ray Harper, spotted them and immediately opened fire. In this short but intense action, Lance Corporal Jorge Wilson distinguished himself for his aggressiveness. Lance Corporal Wilson, originally from Mexico, is a clerk/driver for the FLC legal office when he is not serving as a rifleman/machine gunner with the Provisional Rifle Company. He is a smooth-faced, cheerful young Marine, but his determination to close with the enemy this night forced them to terminate their attack on the Army compound abruptly and to withdraw.

10 December 1968

Last night, while in the COC, I listened to the radio transmissions of a patrol from Charlie Company, First Battalion, Twenty-sixth Marines just across the river from where a Provisional Rifle Company patrol had been the prior night. They saw some black hats moving near the river and sent two squads on line to sweep through the area. The NVA were lying chest deep in an adjacent swamp and ambushed them. The squad leader excitedly relayed to his platoon commander that he was surrounded. A helicopter came in, loaded six of their wounded on it, but then took off without picking up all their wounded. Their corpsman was dead, lying within the killing zone, while the NVA were making fire-team rushes to get his body. Illumination finally came in, enabling the Marines to drive the enemy off, crawl out, and re-

Lance Corporal Jorge Wilson, clerk/driver for the Force Logistics Command legal office by day and rifleman/machine gunner by night. His aggressive action the night of 6 December 1968 forced a VC mortar unit to break off its attack.

trieve the body. They then pulled back and called in an 81 mm mortar mission on the ambush site. We have been fortunate to be spared such actions.

19 December 1968

The company has just returned from a successful two-day operation, which was based on an intelligence tip. On December 17 and 18 we conducted a cordon and search of the village of Ap Trung Son and swept Hill 12 to the south of it, which is an elevated piece of flat, sandy terrain studded with scrub brush. Other than looking for VC suspects in the village, we were searching for concealed bunkers and tunnels in the hill. In the process we found two buried bunker complexes, three VC, and assorted caches. We came prepared. Gene Schwartzlow, the Second Platoon commander, has experience in locating tunnels from his prior duty on the DMZ. There he had worked with Marines to discover tunnels concealed from casual observation. He showed us how to spread out with metal rods and then to move slowly across an area on line, probing for hidden underground spaces while listening for noises indicating that a hollow area lay beneath the surface. As a result, each of our Marines carried a long metal probe.

Ap Trung Son with Hill 12 and graveyard behind it.

Force Logistics Command Marine probing for hidden tunnels at Ap Trung Son, December 1968.

We dispersed so that our movements would be less obvious. First Platoon departed from the adjacent artillery battery compound at 11:00 PM. The Second and Third platoons departed through Gate 4 at FLC at 10:00 PM the same evening. By 4:00 AM on December 18, the cordon of Ap Trung Son was complete. James Petersen, with his Third Platoon, quietly guided the company into its preplanned positions in the dark with a minimum of confusion. Third Platoon spearheaded the cordon of the village. The Vietnamese National Police and the Fifth Counterintelligence team arrived by helicopter at Ap Trung Son at 6:45 AM.

Immediately on the arrival of the Vietnamese police, the villagers were called from their homes by loudspeakers and moved to the village schoolhouse for interrogation. While this was under way, Marines and National Police went through each house from top to bottom. The house searches did not reveal anything of value.

By nine in the morning the focus shifted to Hill 12 behind Ap Trung Son. Lanes were first laid out with engineering tape, and then Gene Schwartzlow's Second Platoon went on line and slowly probed its way across Hill 12, following the taped lanes. The other two platoons provided security.

At approximately 9:45 AM Lance Corporal Melville Butt, Second Platoon, discovered the first buried bunker. The top was blown off with C-4 explosives, and then a detailed search was made of it. No enemy personnel or weapons were found—only one U.S. metal canteen and one U.S. flashlight. The area obviously had been recently inhabited, however, because bamboo air vents were found with fresh grass and leaves that served to purify the air. More important, the smell of human body odor was still apparent. The bamboo bunker was then destroyed with demolitions.

A detailed search was conducted around the first bunker, which led to the discovery of one Chicom grenade and one U.S. flashlight in a nearby garden plot. One bandoleer of M-14 rifle ammunition was also found in a nearby grave site. The sweep of Hill 12 continued.

At 11:00 AM Lance Corporal Gieb, Second Platoon, found the next bunker with three VC inside. Probing with his long metal rod, Gieb heard a hollow echo when his rod struck the top of another enemy bunker buried under the sand. When the top layer of sand was scraped off, a trap door was found. Gieb reached down to pull it up. When he felt someone pushing up from inside at the same time, he dropped the covering and stepped back. We knew we had something. We anticipated that the first thing the VC would do when we pulled back the door would be to throw out a grenade. So we attached a grappling hook to the door, stepped back, and pulled on the grappling hook. Up came the door and out popped a Chicom grenade, which exploded without hurting anyone. Then, a VC opened up with an AK-47.

The VC held his rifle up from within the bunker and tried to spray the area surrounding the bunker door. I could clearly see the muzzle blasts from the assault rifle. When this happened, I think that everyone in the near vicinity went a little crazy. Men ran up, threw themselves down, and set up machine guns, while others returned fire with M-16s. One man squirmed up and threw in a fragmentation grenade. The VC must have had a grenade pit dug in the bottom of their bunker because none appeared to be hurt by the blast and they opened fire again. By this time some Marines were so eager that they had to be pulled back out of the way physically so that they were not in the line of fire.

I vaguely recall being hot and sweaty, because the temperature was in the 90s, and tasting smoke and tear gas. The VC who died in that position did not die pleasantly. The men had apparently hidden in the bunker about twelve hours earlier when we moved in and waited in that confined area all morning, listening as we slowly probed the hill, blew the other bunker/tunnel in place, blew a booby trap in place, and finally stopped over their hiding place.

Only after the second tear gas grenade was tossed in did the first VC pop out with his hands held high. He was vomiting and stumbling, and one of my interrogators knocked him down and pulled him out of the way. He told us that there were two more in the hole but refused to talk them out. With this, the South Vietnamese National Police who were working with us went back in the village and brought out two men whom they forced to approach the bunker in order to talk the VC out. These same men, along with the rest of the village, had stated earlier that there were no VC in the area and that they knew nothing. Nevertheless, the other VC refused to surrender. We were then out of tear gas grenades, so we improvised. I took red, yellow, and green smoke grenades and crawled up to the opening and threw them in. After the first smoke grenade dropped inside the confined space, one VC started out. His head and upper body were emerging when the Marine who was immediately behind me cut him down with his shotgun. It seemed as if every hair on the head of the VC stood straight up, and then he fell back inside. The other man then made up his mind to die in the hole, and he started firing again. I threw in two more yellow smoke grenades, hoping that he would surrender, but he would not and suffocated to death. Each time a fragmentation grenade, tear gas, or smoke grenade was thrown in, the VC responded by firing from their bunker. The VC who was fortunate enough to surrender did so only after raising his hands and signaling that he was surrendering. The VC who was shot tried to come out of the bunker without raising his arms or calling out that he meant to give up.

About this time, it became amazing how aggressive the South Vietnamese became. One jumped down in the hole and put nooses around the necks of the two VC while his buddies pulled them out. Later, I found that a South Vietnamese soldier was attempting to sneak away with one of the Russian pistols found in the second bunker, which I wanted to go to the Marine who discovered the hiding place. I grabbed the pistol from him.

In this action, two Navy corpsmen deserve mention. Hospital Corpsman Third Class Johnny Cox most likely saved the life of the first VC who came out of the bunker after being teargassed. Petty Officer Cox first flushed his mouth out with water and then gave him mouth-to-mouth resuscitation until his breathing was reestablished.

Petty Officer Cox also tried to help the VC who elected to stay in his bunker and succumbed to the gas and the pungent smoke off the smoke grenades. Despite the overpowering odor of gas on the VC, Cox attempted to resuscitate the man by removing mucous from his breathing passage and applying mouth-to-mouth resuscitation. Cox was briefly successful in restarting the man's pulse, but the VC went into shock and died.

Assisting Petty Officer Cox was another corpsman, Hospital Corpsman Third Class Terry Carmoney. Carmoney alternated with Cox in providing care to the wounded Vietnamese.

After the action was over, we recovered two 9 mm pistols and one AK-47; propaganda leaflets; a loudspeaker; a cartridge belt with ammunition for both the pistols and the rifle; rain gear; food; clothing; individual medical supplies; North and South Vietnamese currency; and documents. When we had removed all the contents, we blew up the bunker. Before we left we brought the villagers up and made them look at the bodies. When I returned to base, I slept for fourteen hours.

Note: The person captured was a Viet Cong planner and an executioner. He was responsible for the kidnapping of a Vietnamese student nurse who worked at the nearby artillery battery base and for the execution of her father. He also executed a local hamlet chief favorable to the Saigon regime. Fifth Counterintelligence also informed us that, following the initial interrogation of the VC prisoner and based on information learned from him, the Twenty-sixth Marines mounted an operation, including air strikes, on a hidden VC bunker complex. This operation resulted in one main-force company commander killed along with six Viet Cong main-force soldiers.

The VC in the bunker had belonged to the Viet Cong for many years. One of the dead VC was a sergeant and had eight years of service with the Viet Cong. The other VC had been a member of the Viet Cong for six years, but his rank was unknown. They were in Ap Trung Son with orders to increase local activity against our patrols and to participate in the coming attack on Da Nang.

24 December 1968

Two nights ago at 5:30 PM a small observation helicopter from the Army took off from the Army helicopter pad across the road from us on the way back to its unit. It decided to buzz one of the tall Armed Forces Radio antennas at FLC. In the middle of its turn, it became entangled in the support wires of the antennas, lost its blades, and spun into the swamp behind our officers' club. The pilot, a nineteen-year-old warrant officer, and a sergeant were killed.

Yesterday, I hitchhiked to the Freedom Hill PX and heard Billy Graham preach in the open-air amphitheater. He is a very powerful and emotional preacher. Today, I returned to the same amphitheater to watch the Bob Hope show. He had Miss World, Ann Margaret, and a bevy of other young lovelies. I did not have a seat and was so high on a nearby hill that the show looked like it was being put on by ants, but it was still a thrill. Bob Hope was risqué and funny.

25 December 1968

My first Christmas away from home. I opened my packages today and had one laugh after another. My wonderful family sent so many little trick gifts and knickknacks. I tore into them with gusto and was very grateful for their gestures. Christmas makes a brave try over here, but it seems alien to Vietnam and a war zone. There are 365 days until a real Christmas. Last night I watched a fantastic display of tracers and flares. The sky was filled with red, green, and white flares and red tracers. Later, some of the troops, filled with Christmas cheer, began firing their rifles in the air. I had to dispatch roving patrols to round them up. We finally quieted things down after midnight, and I realized I had missed my first midnight church service in years. All I want now is to get through this year and into 1969.

15 / Bringing in the New Year

2 January 1969

I am now into the last half of my tour. On New Year's Eve I went on patrol with fellow lawyer Jack Provine, who wants to join the Provisional Rifle Company. We crept onto an island with an old pagoda and burial mounds, set up machine guns, calculated fields of fire, spread the riflemen in a 360° security circle, and set out to await the dawn of a brilliant new year and/or the VC. We had a starlight scope with us that penetrated the gloom and turned the night into day. Jack and I paced about under the towering, crooked, and ancient trees, looking for movement around us. No one appeared, but during the night we observed lanterns and small lights blinking mysteriously from first one side of the paddies and then the next. Once a lantern appeared that was held at chest height and was waved in a circle. The bearer then raced off down an unseen trail. At precisely midnight, flares began to pop and soar and flash across the skies, proclaiming boldly a proud new year. About dawn, we shrugged off the fatigue from our eyelids and the chill in our bones and headed back to camp. Several times we heard whistling noises that were nothing like the bird sounds common to our area. It was an excellent patrol, despite the lack of contact. The next day the South Vietnamese ran a sweep in the area and discovered two VC who had burrowed under the very pagoda where we had set up our ambush site. While we were so diligently scanning the fields and tree lines for movement, they were crouching beneath us all the time. Jack and I have told and retold the story many times to the other FLC lawyers, embellishing it and making it funnier each time.

7 January 1969

I seemed to go through the rest of the week in a mechanical routine, stuck in an unimaginative cycle. I sat as the president of a special court-martial where we found the defendant guilty and gave him six months' confinement at hard labor and forfeitures of forty-five dollars a month for six months. The commanding officer of Fifth Communications Battalion was grateful because he believed that this example would help discipline.

Jack Provine, as defense counsel, and I, as government counsel, then went to Dong Ha to try another special court. Private Fred Lindemuller looked like a fresh-faced innocent child, but the mere mention of his name sent everyone from his sergeant up to the camp commander into sputtering fits. He was a shrewd little con man who constantly went to the edge of the law (or past it) but could never be pinned down. This time his luck ran out, and he was convicted of disrespect, disobedience of lawful orders, and assault. Bravo (Dong Ha) has had some severe disciplinary problems even though it is essentially a small and close-knit command. Glen Myers (my good friend and the battalion legal officer and adjutant) had a hand grenade rolled under his hut when he put too much pressure on a local pot-blowing group. Somehow he escaped injury. This could not be tolerated, and discipline had to be enforced.

The court was the reflection of the command's determination to get tough on offenders. It was composed of ex-enlisted officers with apparently hundreds of years of prior service under their belts. When Jack questioned the court to see whether there were any grounds for challenge, they all answered his questions as if each was the epitome of wisdom and fair play, elaborately taking time to answer questions and ponderously thinking out their unimpeachably fair answers. Jack removed the colonel who was in charge of the court in order to shake up the composition of the personalities—but it did not change the outcome. The remaining members of the court quickly arrived at a verdict. Private Lindemuller was found guilty and given four months' confinement in the brig and four months' forfeiture in pay.

I believe the high point of the trip was taking a ride by convoy to Vande-

Jack Provine at Vandergrif Combat Base.

grif Combat Base in the DMZ. Glen took his jeep, and, with Jack and me riding shotgun, acting as forward observers, and seeking adventure, we rolled out of Dong Ha, heading north. We drove full speed through a constant cloud of fine, powdery dust. I felt as if the country was familiar. This was the area where Jim Brown fought his war and was wounded. The convoy never slowed down for fear of being ambushed. We wound past huts of displaced Montagnards, peasant Vietnamese, past rugged hills of solid rocky crags and intermittent tree lines (which would be hell to take in an assault—and which the Marines took by assault), past slow-running ribbons of jungle water and lush vegetation, and past destroyed bridges and isolated outposts, and then, lickety-split, down the valley road and through the last hills into Vandegrif Combat Base. Vandegrif is our advanced combat base, headquarters of Task Force Hotel and hub of maneuvering infantry battalions that are constantly radiating out from and sweeping the mountains, remote valleys, and forests for the North Vietnamese. Today, the enemy is being coy, and it is a time of lull; not too many days before, it had been business as usual, and the graves registration teams had worked overtime. The base is well dug in by the engineers, with bunkers deep underground. It is in a valley with a long airplane and helicopter runway plowed out of the dirt and dominated all the way around by not-so-far-away mountain ridges that we presumably dominate. The "grunts" stage here in tents staked out on dry, dusty earth in an-ticipation of being helilifted in the never-ending operations. Artillery and mortar crews are in sandbagged emplacements surrounded by their handi-work of empty shell casings. Helicopter noises and swirling blades fill the sky as the sleek machines dart back and forth like agitated dragonflies.

16 / R&R Down Under

Finally! My R&R date arrived. On 14 January 1969, I reported to the R&R center at Freedom Hill to go to the continent down under. It is amazing, on driving away from base with orders and bags packed, how much the spirits are lifted. It was a happy exhilaration accompanied by an intense feeling that the sky was bluer, that the grass was greener, and that life was infinitely richer. My next feeling was of bone-deep weariness.

The trip was swift on the Boeing 707 jet. We had live American stewardesses, who treated the patient masses with a superior, understanding tolerance, allowing us all to gaze on their unspeakable beauty and think unthinkable thoughts.

On arrival in Sydney, after a brief layover in Darwin, we were bundled into buses and taken to the R&R center, where we were briefed on how to handle ourselves, what to wear, what not to do, and where we should not go, and we were warned of dire military consequences if we did any of a number of things ("Number 1, don't make an ass out of yourself.").

I checked into the Menzies Hotel, one of the finest lodging establishments in Sydney, and set out with the determination of American genius to spend all my money. I traveled alone, which enabled me to meet people more easily if the stars were right, but without another person to talk to and do things with, it was more difficult to relax and come out of one's shell and get back into the real world. I found myself embarrassingly and uncharacteristically tongue-tied for the first two days. But the Australians would not let me feel like an outsider; I met some of the finest and most gracious people I have ever had the pleasure to know. On my second morning I screwed up my courage to do one of those educational tasks that one sets for himself, and I went to call on an Australian firm of solicitors (lawyers). I delayed as long as possible and then picked some names out of the phone book in the heart of the economic center of Pitt Street and set off. The first firm that I went to see had most of its personnel either on summer vacation or out to lunch ("tough beans, drop in again the next time you're in Australia"). I walked downstairs and decided to try one more firm in the building. The firm was Walter Dickson and Company. The receptionist went scurrying off to see whether any respectable attorney had time to spend on an American who just stumbled through the door. Mr. Dev Webber is a senior partner and one of those rare individuals with a keen imagination, driving intellect, and a delightful sense of humor that caught me completely by surprise. I did not realize my good fortune as I entered the office. The offices are not luxurious compared to most modern American standards. Their law is more generalized and less specialized than in the United States, with more of an accent on the personal touch between firm and client and less of the atmosphere of a law factory. Dev was immediately inquisitive and friendly and told me about their methods of practice in Australia and flattered me by drawing on my shallow knowledge of U.S. private practice. I kept looking at my watch, fearing I was keeping Dev past his lunch, when he asked me to dine with him. We ate in what had been traditionally an old club in the economic and marketing center of Pitt Street, and before we parted he invited me to join his family the coming Sunday at their summer house on the bay for a day of sailing. I accepted and had one of the happiest days of my life.

Dev had his relatives, Ruth and Peter Flood, vacationing at their house with their beautiful blond-haired children. Peter ranches in the outback and only once a year comes to the city, or its outskirts, to relax. Peter and Dev met me in their sailboat to take me up the beautiful inlet to their cove, where their house is nestled on the side of a steep hill tucked under tall trees. The inlets and tree-studded hills reminded me of Maine, but the Webbers' keen hospitality was pure Aussie. There was a group of young people as well who had come to work and live in Australia. We first grabbed the mob of children, piled in the local fire chief's jeep, and went for a drive up a narrow, rutted trail, all hanging on, part in and part out, to get the best views of the area. Dev pointed out remote back areas where convict labor had been originally used and a cave where a well-known convict once hid. Then we went back to the house, down to the boat, and out for a sail and swim. It was a perfect day. The boys found a small octopus, which we chased in our boat. The water was so clear that the octopus appeared to be only a few feet deep when it was more likely ten feet under. When we sailed into the lagoon beach area for a swim, the other boats that were enjoying a quiet, relaxing afternoon upped anchors and fled. Later, we returned to the house for lunch and good company. When late afternoon finally stalked the hills, it was time to go. I felt a keen regret, as if I were leaving my own family.

There were so many kind people, and it was such a delicious rest—what a complete change of scenery. It seemed that every time I went into a restaurant or bar, someone would come up and poke a smiling face in mine and take off in conversation. People came up to me on the streets and asked whether I was enjoying myself. The girls in their beautiful short minidresses were tanned, firm, and friendly.

17 / Back to Reality

28 January 1969

While I was enjoying the bliss of R&R, VC sappers cut their way through the perimeter wire of our base, penetrated inside, blew up some paint and other minor supplies, and escaped with no casualties on either side. Obviously, the VC were only probing us and training their cadre on how easy it is to get into FLC. Perhaps they will come back later for the real show. The sad truth is that one of my patrols spotted them moving through the tree line on the way in and requested permission to open fire. It was denied, and they were directed to continue on their patrol.

Pete Mastaglio told me that when the sirens went off announcing an attack and he heard small-arms fire, he immediately suspected that VC had come through the wire and were on base. He decided that it made more sense to stay out of the way and to get into his bunker. When he made this suggestion to John Reilly, John said, "Hell, no!" pulled out his .45 pistol, chambered a round, and stalked off in the darkness ready to repel boarders.

The night before last, I was returning to my hut after enjoying a going-away party for Ron Williamson when First Lieutenant Bob Walker, my new executive officer for the rifle company, came in and said our patrol was in contact. I threw my clothes on and raced to the COC in time to hear the excited voices of the radiomen saying that they had two enemy killed in action and were continuing contact. The patrol caught the VC moving through the islands and drainage canals in the paddies. They spotted a group of six, set in a hasty ambush, and opened fire on them. The VC dropped back into a canal and attempted to evade my Marines. The patrol then ran down to the other end of the canal and caught them as they were coming out, pouring M-16 fire and M-79 rounds into them. The VC (later found to be NVA) left two dead floating in the muddy paddy, and first light revealed large blood smears going back down the side of the canal as the enemy dragged themselves or were dragged away. The leeches were already in the fresh blood. Extensive searches were conducted by the South Vietnamese Army and combined action units that day for wounded NVA in the villages or fresh graves, but nothing turned up. The patrol also spotted another group of twenty-three enemy, took them under fire, and turned them back from their destination of either FLC or Da Nang.

By radio from the COC, I directed another patrol to move to Ap Trung Son and to secure it from sniper fire in order to provide cover for the patrol already in contact in the paddies. I dispatched another patrol to assist the one in contact and to sweep the area for enemy casualties and equipment (again we had no casualties). We then obtained the use of a helicopter from the Army and lifted a squad behind what I hoped would be the enemy's line of retreat. There was an awkward moment at first. When the helicopter arrived at the pad, the pilot asked where the G-3 (intelligence officer) was because he was ready for his briefing. There was no time for formalities. I pulled out my map, turned on my flashlight, and said, "Listen carefully, I am about to give you your briefing." Then I told him where the enemy was last reported and where we needed to be let off. We shuttled in two loads; I took in the original group of nine men. Eight more came in afterward. We rendezvoused on an island, expecting fire, but there was none. We then deployed some people, hoping to catch any groups trying to retreat through our sector. Nevertheless, the night passed uneventfully, although we had to dodge mortar illumination canisters that were impacting only feet from us.

I was tired and kept trying to fight fatigue and sleep. Gradually the dawn broke in red streaks with a deep richness of color tinted by a light haze off the paddies. The unbelievably beautiful fresh green of the tropic vegetation was punctuated by the movement of Marine squads sweeping the area for the enemy.

The enemy dead had NVA uniforms on, carried NVA currency, and had safe-conduct passes through our area directed to the local VC. They looked like teenage boys to me.

There is one image stamped on my memory from this encounter. Walking along the path a short distance from the enemy bodies, while the day was still fresh and full of promise, I found a human brain lying on the ground. Pink and out of place, the vision of that misplaced portion of a human being still returns to me.

2 February 1969

Last night our neighboring unit of Seabees, NCB-22, gave a farewell party prior to rotating home. Because I have defended several Seabees, I was asked to attend, and Colonel Haden, Major Moore, Captain Provine, and Captain Schwindt from FLC were also included. We enjoyed ourselves excessively. I took liberal advantage of their open bar, and soon all of us were in grand spirits. General J. A. Feeley Jr. from FLC was also there. When I was introduced to him again, he made some polite references to my work with the Provisional Rifle Company. Later, when I showed up at the bar for another scotch and water, the good general half seriously said, "Captain Griffis, don't you think you should go easy on that? What if you have to be called out again tonight?" Equal to the occasion, I blurted out, "Don't worry, General, I am always ready to go!" grabbed my drink, and slid back into the crowd. Before the night was over, Tom Schwindt cornered the general and convinced him that Tom wanted to be a pilot. The general agreed to contact all his friends in Headquarters, U.S. Marine Corps, to arrange it, and I kept saying that I wanted to make a career as an infantry officer in the Marine Corps. The next morning, both of us were afraid that General Feeley would remember to whom he was talking. We did not return to FLC until after midnight when, after wrestling Jack Provine to the ground, I made it to bed.

4 February 1969

Yesterday we paid our respects to Private First Class Alvin Derrick, Third Platoon, Provisional Rifle Company, in a simple but moving ceremony. His rifle was stuck bayonet first in sandbags with his helmet hanging on it. We sang "The Battle Hymn of the Republic" and heard the quiet, sincere words of Chaplain Goad. Then taps was played. The heart-wrenching piece seemed to go through my soul and left me shivering.

Derrick was an easygoing eighteen-year-old boy from South Carolina. Out on patrol, his squad had been moving through the islands after dawn, walking down a main dike along the rice paddies. The first six men had crossed over a small bamboo bridge, and Sergeant Parker, the squad leader, was already around a corner of another island when there was a loud detonation. Private First Class Derrick, the seventh man, stepped on an explosive pressure device that blew him about fifteen meters off the dike into the rice paddy and tossed his machine gun into the air like a broken toy. The people around froze, and Sergeant Parker took off running to help when he saw Derrick's body lying in the water. When Sergeant Parker grabbed him, he realized that Derrick was already dead and, mercifully, never knew what had hit him. The platoon was shocked to the marrow. For the next few days, we kept the men so busy that they did not have time to think and were ready to drop from exhaustion. Now they have rebounded and have accepted their loss. What they need is some kind of action. This steady diet of grinding patrols and training will take its toll.

For the rest of the week, I took the company out several days for intensive training at the South Vietnamese Army boot camp beyond the III Marine Amphibious Force brig, where we fired all our weapons, mortars, machine guns, laws (light anti-tank weapons), rifles, claymore mines, and M-79s. Then on Sunday we kicked off Operation Co-Op with First Battalion, Twenty-sixth Marines in one of the largest operations I have known in our area. It involved elements of three battalions and other commands in a cordon and search of Ap Nam O, thought to be the closest and biggest storage area for the VC in the northern Da Nang sector. I moved out with the First Platoon as part of the cordon and search at 12:00 AM on the chilly Asian morning of 9 February. We were in position by our allotted time of 4:00 AM, but this was the last thing that went right. Shortly thereafter, First Platoon opened fire on people moving into our sector along the beach. Actually, they were elements of B Company, First Battalion, Twenty-sixth Marines who were drifting into the beach area to close a gap but who neglected to tell us. One of them was shot through both legs. Later in the day, recriminations flew through the area, with the colonel of the First Battalion,

Twenty-sixth Marines ordering a formal investigation, accompanied with vile mutterings about the competency of my people. There was a swell of relief as the headquarters' personnel of the First Battalion, Twenty-sixth Marines ultimately realized their own troops had been in error for coming down the beach without informing us.

My troops experienced more back luck. The local Vietnamese told us that the VC had heard the day before of our coming and had already left. We found some rice and a few suspects but little else other than beer and Popsicle stands waiting for us. One of my men was gored in his right buttock by an irate water buffalo. What an inglorious way to go—carried from the field on a stretcher, laid low by a Communist water buffalo.

18 / Looking for Trouble

On the fifteenth of February, I went out with a daylight patrol to try out a different approach to an ambush and to show the troops that I was not bothered by the threat of booby traps—so, somehow, they need not be either. This, of course, was a lie. The squad went out in the afternoon, and my plan was for us to make ourselves seen, leading the Vietnamese into thinking that this was our one patrol for the day. We went through the villages along the rice paddies, wound through the middle of Ap Trung Son, and then headed north to the islands as sunset crept over the countryside. The patrol entered one of the islands and set up 360° security. I then handpicked three men to join me. We painted ourselves with camouflage greasepaint, taped down our baggy trousers and anything that clinked, stuffed our pockets with grenades and flares, and checked our weapons, radio, and starlight scope. I briefed them again on our mission.

After dark, the patrol would depart and head back for base, stumbling along the narrow, tottering rice paddy dikes, slipping off and splashing into the paddies, and generally act in our normal crafty fashion. When the patrol reached a depression in the sand near to FLC, it would pause, and three Marines and I would shed our bulky flak jackets and helmets. After the patrol had popped its green star clusters and proceeded normally back into the camp, the four of us would circle back into the rice paddies. All went according to plan.

The plan was that we would silently crawl through the mud, wade along in the canals like Viet Cong, and enter Ap Trung Son at the rear of the village. We would then try to find the three VC who we had been told by intelligence were holed up in tunnels. They were known to have planted booby traps and propagandized the villagers by night.

Four people is a small group to be out alone in enemy territory, but I figured that if we ran into anything big, I would probably be able to call in mortar fire with the radio. For a change, we had the element of surprise because the VC would not be expecting us. We also had a starlight scope and stopped every few minutes to listen and search the area. Everything went beautifully. It was pitch-black dark, and we took seven hours to crawl seven hundred meters. I had the point man in front of me, then myself for control, and the radioman behind me; another rifleman with the starlight scope brought up the rear. We never walked, but stayed in the paddies, slithering along on our bellies or crawling on our hands and knees. Every fifty meters I stopped the group to listen for unusual sounds. We did not merely listen; we strained to hear until our heads ached, and then we moved on. Keeping only our rifles and heads out of the water and freezing every time a flare lit up the sky, we waded in the canals. We endured sucking leeches and jabbing mosquitoes, but our efforts were rewarded. No one knew we were there.

Every other time I had been on a night patrol, our presence had been telegraphed by lights that sprang up as we moved from one village to another. Answering lights would then flicker on and off as if a breeze were blowing a bush in front of them. This would occur even when there was no breeze, and, when flickering lights were seen, we were rarely rewarded with contact. There were lights all around us tonight, but they had a clear, steady beam. With our starlight scope, we saw a man sneak out of Ap Trung Son, go to one of the islands, squat down, and set a booby trap. All that time, another light beamed the steady all clear from the tree line of Ap Trung Son. I directed the point to swing further south so that we could crawl into Ap Trung Son from the rear and get a crack at the local talent with their lights. By this time, we had been crawling about six hours, and Lance Corporal Henson, the point, was tired and nervous and beginning to make too much noise for my comfort. Visions of the cadavers we had made of the VC a few weeks ago in these same paddies kept coming into my brain. Derrick died again, and I knew more than anything else I wanted to live and go home. I signaled Henson to drop behind me, and I took the point. About ten minutes later, we thought we heard a rustling in the reeds. We froze. Nothing. We moved another seventy-five meters. We were crawling along the edge of a dike toward the intersection with a canal when I heard sloshing sounds moving toward us in the canal. I motioned everyone down into a hasty ambush, signaled Henson to get a grenade ready to throw on my command, and indicated to everyone else to prepare to spray the area with our M-16s. Lance Corporal C. W. Wozniewski, the rifleman, then signaled that he saw two and then eight figures through the starlight scope. The noises drew closer; I wanted them to be right on us before we fired. Then I heard what sounded like the clinking of equipment, and I began to fear we might be taking on more than we could handle. Before I knew it, there were sounds both behind us and coming toward us; one or more of them had already slipped past. I prayed to God for what I was about to do. Then I motioned Henson to throw his grenade at the sounds that had passed by. When the explosion went off, I opened up on automatic toward the other end of the canal. I was astonished when a burst hit near us coming from Ap Trung Son. I heard "Ski" and the radioman fire into the northern end of the village at the same time. We popped flares and attempted a quick search of the area, but in the stark light of the flares, everything seemed unreal. Nothing moved; I saw no signs of the enemy. I called in illumination rounds from our 81 mm mortars at FLC, and we spread out to search the area. It was at this time that I discovered that the people Ski had spotted were not coming at us down the canal but rather were standing farther off in the tree line near the signal light in Ap Trung Son. They were in uniform with full military equipment but could not have been the source of the sounds in the water next to us. Ski and the radioman had fired at the people in the tree line while Henson and I had opened fire on the noises in the canal closer to us. Because we were low in the paddies, the troops in Ap Trung Son could not locate us and had returned fire to my left before scattering. By this time, the mortars began dropping illumination right on target, but the canisters were falling within fifty meters of us. The mortar men fired three rounds, but then the gun went down, leaving us shrouded in darkness. In our brief minutes of sunshine, I discovered that Ski's M-16 was jammed, that the starlight scope had gone out, and that we were low on ammo. The illumination had not revealed any enemy close to us but had revealed to them that there were only four of us. We reassembled at this point, and I decided that it was time for us to go home. It had taken us seven hours to crawl out there, but the trip back to FLC went much faster. We were out of the paddies in forty-five minutes and back at base within two hours. Our morale shot up knowing we could roam undetected if we patrolled the hard way and imitated our frontier ancestors. But what did we shoot at in the canal? Instead of attacking the VC, I am afraid that the noises we heard moving in the water were Vietnamese frogs. Frog legs anyone?

19 / Tet 1969 and New Threats

18 February 1969

On 16 February we received word from Fifth Counterintelligence that they had picked up a Chieu Hoi who was willing to lead us to a bunker complex containing his weapon and several other VC. We tried to get the OK to go after them, but the labyrinthine chain of command refused us permission to act. There was a Tet truce in effect from 6:00 PM on 16 February until 6:00 PM on 17 February, and we could only take defensive actions. Semantics! This would be a preventive, defensive act similar to cutting a cancer out of the body, but it was easier in the chain of command to deny approval than to grant it. Third Platoon was prepared to mount out and was disappointed when the mission was scrubbed. We were told that the Vietnamese national police would handle it.

The next day, 17 February (Tet), I was returning from lunch when Bob Walker caught me at the legal office and said, "Skipper, the Vietnamese didn't go out last night, and Fifth Counterintelligence wants us to go with them to make the grab at 6:00 PM."

Great! "Saddle up Third Platoon," I said. "And arrange for helicopters to lift First Squad in by air. The other squads will go out by truck, debark, and get in blocking positions."

The minor problem was that we planned and executed the mission without going through the entire chain of command to get approval. We were told by the Fifth Counterintelligence that there was an opportunity, and I was determined we would seize it. Later, when we brought back the booty, I apologized and said that I thought everyone had been notified and that the operation had been cleared. We coordinated with Fifth Counterintelligence, picked up one of their sergeants, a Vietnamese interpreter, and the Chieu Hoi, and we made our plans. It was then that I first learned we were going to a bunker on Thuy Tu Island, which is not in our tactical area but rather the tactical area of First Battalion, Twenty-sixth Marines. At the last minute, I called to make coordination with First Battalion, Twenty-sixth Marines to let them know we were lifting into their area and then sped off in the truck with my troops to the helipad. At 6:00 PM, we were airborne in two choppers and soon were circling the island.

We dropped down to an open field in a beautifully green tropical setting bathed in honey yellow by the slowly setting sun. Several men moved out to set up security, and we headed off with the ex-VC to find his hole. It was at the base of a hedge between two banana trees under boards and dirt. We fanned out to cover the entrance while personnel from the Fifth Counterintelligence shoved the Chieu Hoi forward to talk his mates out. As I watched the thin, scared little man edge nervously up to the entrance of the tunnel, I was overcome by a feeling of disgust at the idea of living in a hole scratched in the dirt like an animal. No one appeared to be home, so we threw in tear gas to check for sure. Then one of my men, Gatz, the Marine who so long ago I wrote up for stealing a baby duck while on patrol, put on a gas mask, took a flashlight, and snaked into the hole. Soon he pushed out AK-47 and AK-50 Communist assault rifles along with bags of food, clothing, medicine, and uniforms. We found two large propaganda banners with yellow letters on a red background that were made to be strung across the highway. One proclaimed, "Freedom for the Vietnamese People," and the other stated, "Americans, get out of Viet-Nam and let the Vietnamese settle their own problems." We found a red and blue silk Viet Cong flag and a red flag with a big gold hammer and sickle in the center of it. There were Chicom hand grenades, a booby trap, and, most important, a bag of documents. We placed demolitions in the hole and blew it wider and then found another AK-47 rifle with more bags of equipment and food. What a grand haul! Poor Gatz, though, was sprawled on the ground in real pain. As he was backing out of the tunnel his gas mask had caught on a piece of debris that pulled the mask down and exposed his face and lungs to the gas. The demolition further spread gas over the area so that we were all contaminated from it as we went through the saturated booty. Gatz had to be led back to the landing zone with his hands on the shoulders of another Marine, but he quickly recovered. It was dark when we finally signaled the helicopters in for the pickup, and we were soon back at the base.

Predictably, the command of First Battalion, Twenty-sixth Marines was outraged that we had penetrated their area and run off with the spoils, and I had some explaining to do to my command. Today I have been in Phu Bai on an article 32 investigation for an upcoming court-martial, so I do not know what the final verdict on our raid will be. I assume that my methods will be disapproved of because I did not wait to let everyone give his approval (which would never have been given because the cache was out of our area), but then the results speak for themselves. I have particularly high hopes that the documents will turn out to be of value and might contain the Communists' plans for Tet in our area. It is too bad that we did not find the Chieu Hoi's friends at home and scoop them in as well. I am tired, and it seems like June is oh so far away!

23 February 1969

The long-anticipated Tet offensive has now been under way for about twenty-four hours. We were hit by 122 mm and 140 mm rockets at 2:00 AM, 5:30 AM, and again at 9:00 AM. There was heavy contact all over the area throughout the night. The deep-water pier across the harbor rocked with explosions through the night and into the morning as fuel and ammunition dumps went up. Sappers also got into the South Vietnamese Army ammo dump and blew it. The VC have played cat and mouse inside Da Nang today, and a twenty-four-hour curfew has been set for everyone. A Marine company on Hill 240 was overrun early this morning, and a call went out for volunteers here to help carry the bodies in. At about 11:30 AM today, we heard that Observation Post Eagle, on one of the ridges south of us, was being overrun and had VC in the protective concertina wire. Still, the enemy has yet to commit the bulk of its troops. We are waiting to see what will develop tonight.

This morning I received a call from Northern Sector Defense Command to pick up the platoon attached to the Provisional Rifle Company from Seventh Engineer Battalion and bring it to the headquarters of First Marine Division, where it is to participate as part of a reaction force. VC were in spider holes in a village nearby, and a joint Vietnamese/U.S. Marine force was organized to sweep them out. I grabbed Sergeant Burns from the COC and went to Seventh Engineers to pick up their people. They gradually put their gear together and loaded up their trucks; we then took off with my jeep in the lead. As we were weaving around the valley road and headed down the straight stretch of road toward Eleventh Motors and First Division's headquarters, 122 mm rockets began to "kerump" in the adjacent fields. The white/gray splashes of smoke erupted in quick succession in the field to my right and then walked across the road in front of us as we were driving. I told Sergeant Burns to step on it and try to speed through the danger area, but two more rounds hit close to us. We skidded to a halt next to a ditch. The first truck with its troops slammed to a stop close behind us; there was a mass exodus of people hurtling the sides of the truck and scrambling and crawling for the ditch. One young heavily loaded Marine hauled past me, caught his bedroll in the barbed wire running along the ditch, and fell with a thud as white feathers from the bedroll scattered everywhere. For a moment, I felt detached from the explosions and the rush of bodies around me. I helped the Marine get up and assured him that we would all be okay. When there was a lull, we loaded up again and sped the rest of the way to First Division. On the way, we passed a jeep stranded in the middle of the road with its tires shot out as several Marines ran over to pull out the limp form of another Marine from behind the wheel. I left the platoon at First Division's headquarters and returned to FLC to see what else developed.

I will digress for a moment. We have had steady contact for the last three days. Three days ago, the Chieu Hoi who took us into Thuy Tu Island to scoop up that cache led a squad from the rifle company to a bunker south of Ap Nam O where more VC and equipment were supposed to be. The squad took cover behind a stone wall while the South Vietnamese Army interpreter tried to talk the VC out. Then everything broke loose. The VC shot the interpreter through the chest and began throwing out Chicom grenades. The grenades fell behind the wall where my people were and exploded. Eight men were wounded. One Marine (Private Gatz) had a grenade land next to him while other Marines clustered nearby. Instead of rolling to his own safety, he picked the grenade up and heaved it behind him into the rice paddies, where it exploded and struck him with shrapnel. Our corpsman, who was hit in the leg by fragments, pulled the pieces out himself, crawled up, treated the wounded under fire, and then went out in the rice paddy at a torturous run to revive another man who had collapsed from heat stroke. The Marine stopped breathing before the corpsman reached him, but mouth-to-mouth resuscitation revived him and saved his life. I recommended both the corpsman and Gatz for combat decorations. I hate to say, however, that I finally lost Private Gatz. Gatz, my duck thief, gradually became an outstanding field Marine and always stayed enthusiastic. He was wounded with shrapnel near his spine and was medivaced to the States. Nevertheless, we were able to promote him to private first class and see that he was awarded a Purple Heart before he was evacuated.

We took another squad out with a VC girl, who led us to some more bunkers. They were old and empty, but she did show us several small caches of grenades she had buried in the sand, one of which was rigged to go off as a booby trap. We blew this in place by putting a grenade next to it and pulling the pin. She also led us to the ammunition for her rifle but conveniently forgot where she had hidden the weapon.

7 March 1969

In the past week, we have had three rocket attacks, two of them on the same evening. We had eight casualties the night we were hit twice, but, again, it is interesting to note that the only seriously wounded were hit with shrapnel from the waist up. The moral of the story is to hit the ground and crawl when the air fills with foreign objects. Lieutenant Colonel Morris attempted to run from his hut when he heard the first rounds slam into the area and received multiple wounds from flying shrapnel. A flying nail that had been torn out of a board injured his spine. In the meantime, our area remains relatively free of ground action. The patrols have occasional brushes with the enemy, but now we are awaiting 15 March (the ides of March), when the enemy's major ground offensive is supposed to be launched.

We also have another enemy to face. There is an intense, vicious, but effective program of Communist propaganda in the surrounding villages. Our patrols must be hurting them more than we actually know. We hope they are depriving the enemy of easy access to our operations. Perhaps the very fact that the base has not been attacked by mortars since last summer or hit

by any ground forces during this present offensive is because of our effective-
ness. I like to think so. The fact is that, through a smear campaign, the VC
are pushing hard to cost us support and deny us access to their areas. They
are spreading the word that when the Marine patrols come through a village and the men are out in the fields working, the Americans line up the
women of the village and strip-search them. I had this complaint about a
squad from Third Platoon last week and investigated it. The patrol was near-
ing Ap Trung Son from the islands and was in the vicinity of the place where
Private First Class Derrick was killed when they noticed that the Vietnamese
were acting different from usual. All the people, instead of being dispersed
through the fields working, were gathered in one area closely watching the
Americans, as if waiting for something to happen. The Marines became
wary of an ambush or of walking into booby traps, so they motioned several older children to walk in front of them into the village. This seemed to
anger the people.

The patrol did not follow standard procedure, I am told. Instead of passing through with an attempt at friendly conversation with the villagers while
dispensing candy to the kids, they interrogated the villagers through an interpreter. The patrol was attempting to get information on three VC who re-
portedly frequent their village. Also, a local VC cadre leader, Hoa Binh, is
supposedly in the area.

The patrol asked them, "Where are the VC? We know they are in the
area. Tell us, and we will protect you from them. Where is Hoa Binh? We
know he is in the area; show us where."

These questions visibly agitated the people and made them nervous. They
responded with "I don't know" and vague generalities.

The patrol closely checked the papers and clothing of everyone approaching the village along the main paddy dike. They searched through the wom-
en's produce baskets and had the women take down their hair and shake it
out for concealed messages. They searched the seams of the people's clothing for messages, and one girl became hysterical when she saw that her basket was about to be searched. The patrol let her go, but she was probably a
VC messenger. The children in the village acted afraid of the patrol and ran
from them. With hindsight, I think now that when the patrol was approaching the village, the people were probably assembled in one area to give hidden VC free fields of fire for an ambush, but it was likely foiled by the patrol's

having the children proceed in front of them. Undoubtedly, we had come on the village when the VC were there, and our questions and searches were too close to home.

The next day we had a formal protest at FLC from the chief of the village that my people had molested their women and had committed outrages in the village. That charge can be very effective. It made me angry until I fully investigated it. It is a charge calculated to anger any man before the facts are known. Foreigners are molesting your women! Of course, at the same time the good chief denied knowing that any VC were in his village or ever had been.

Our colonel responded with simple language whose meaning could not be misunderstood: "We will fully investigate any complaints against our Marines, but we are not going to stop our patrolling."

Afternoon—I have just been notified that the patrol out this afternoon has triggered a booby trap and that a medivac helicopter has been called. The wounded person is Lance Corporal Henson, the same fine Marine who was the point man when I went with my four-man patrol not long ago. His fire team had moved on to one of the islands to check it out when he exploded a Chicom grenade that was hanging in a tree and rigged to go off waist high. He received multiple shrapnel wounds in his right arm, leg, and side. Although he should recover in time, he will have to be medivaced out of country.

20 / A Life-and-Death Drama

10 March 1969

The night before last was both tense and frustrating. We are now on high alert, with ground attacks expected in our area from 8 March to 15 March. Two battalions of NVA are threatening in our area, and FLC is expected to be challenged with rocket and mortar attacks. With contact imminent, I decided to accompany Sergeant Parker's squad, which was patrolling the northernmost portion of our area and the region adjacent to the tactical area where First Battalion, Twenty-sixth Marines operates.

The patrol moved out. Although I think highly of the abilities of Sergeant Parker, I noticed that his men were tense and showed the effects of their ten nights on ambush duty. We crossed the rice paddy area and gradually moved into an old pagoda and graveyard area located on a small hill to set up an ambush site. In the moonlight we checked the area first for booby traps and then treaded our way up a small path to the top of the hill where patrol headquarters was set up. The other elements moved to their positions from there.

About 11:00 PM there was a loud explosion in the darkness as a claymore mine was detonated; then two more bangs came in a rapid succession. A patrol from First Battalion, Twenty-sixth Marines had sprung its ambush about eight hundred meters west of us. We watched their machine-gun tracers move lazily back and forth through the paddies, probing with red fingers for the enemy. M-79 grenades were fired into the area, along with small-arms fire and a host of illumination rounds. After seven or eight minutes of firing, we could hear voices from the Marine sweep team as they came through the area searching for the enemy, and by the light of the flares, I could clearly observe the Marines with my field glasses. Then came the surprise as Sergeant Parker and I watched the Marines who were on line and sweeping the area. In the light of the flares, I saw a young VC crawling low in the rice paddy, carrying his AK-47. I could see the tension in his face as a big Marine walked just past him with his M-16 at the ready, but the Marine was looking away and did not see him. While the young Vietnamese slowly crawled away to safety, the Marines continued their sweep, calling to each other and covering the area ahead of them with fire. In the glare of the flares, the VC looked young and scared, and the Marines looked big and strong. Life or death was a matter of a few feet. I was simply an onlooker, and we could not risk firing at the VC for fear of hitting the Marines in the area. I also feared that the Marines would mistake us for the enemy and return the fire. Due to a problem with our radio, we were unable to coordinate with the Marine patrol to get them to search farther to their east.

Because the VC was crawling in our direction, we alerted our people to prepare a welcome for him. One fire team leader, Corporal Hughes, had just been up to get directions for his fire team from Sergeant Parker and was moving back down the path when a loud explosion split the air, throwing dust and debris over us. Corporal Hughes had stepped on a mine. I heard him moan twice, and then in a voice that sounded almost normal, he repeated over and over that he was all right. I kept my eyes on the VC and sent the corpsman and Sergeant Parker to see what had happened to Hughes. Retracing his steps over the same path that every one of us had treaded as we filed into the ambush site, Corporal Hughes had the bad luck of stepping on a pressure device. A chunk of earth was scooped out, and fragmentation wounds tore through his body. A flak jacket probably saved his life. A bandoleer of bullets draped across his chest also helped stop the projectiles from hitting his heart. As the first shock of the injury wore off, Hughes lay there, softly repeating how much he hurt. We called in a helicopter medivac for him, and shortly thereafter I watched four Marines, bent double, carry Hughes on his poncho to the chopper. The next day the members of his squad visited him prior to his medivac back to the States. He is expected to recover. Corporal Hughes had twenty-three days left in-country before the explosion.

When Hughes triggered the mine, the VC crawling toward us disappeared. The rest of that night was cold and silent. Wind whipped through the pagoda. I looked out at the full moon, completely depressed at the turn of events.

21 / Murder at Chu Lai

12 March 1969

Today I represented the government in an article 32 investigation into the circumstances surrounding the killing of a first lieutenant (First Lieutenant Earl K. Ziegler) by a corporal (Corporal Charlie Eason III) at Chu Lai. First Lieutenant Ziegler was shot at close range in the mailroom of the First Combined Action Group headquarters shortly before Christmas 1968. Jack Provine was assigned the defense of Corporal Eason. After the investigation was completed, Corporal Eason was referred to a general court-martial for murder.

At first glance I assumed that race was a factor (First Lieutenant Ziegler was white, and Corporal Eason is black, and there had been racial tensions in various units) or that at least there was some prior friction between the two men that led to this shooting. I also assumed that because of this incident Corporal Eason most likely had a prior record of getting into trouble and was a true hard case. Although the facts leave no doubt that the corporal walked into the mailroom where the lieutenant was helping two other Marines sort Christmas mail and coolly fired an entire clip of M-16 tracers into his abdomen and chest, the reasons for this crime are not so clear.

The two Marines who observed this shooting, as well as the two chasers who escorted Corporal Eason to the III Marine Amphibious Force brig outside Da Nang, were called as witnesses. In addition, the headquarters' first sergeant testified to the background events leading up to the murder.

Corporal Eason is a rifleman who has served one tour in Vietnam and then volunteered to extend for a second tour. After his second tour, he then extended for a third tour, which is when this shooting occurred. With each extension, the Marine Corps gave Corporal Eason thirty days' leave, which he could take almost anywhere in the free world at government expense. He took his first thirty-day leave in Baltimore, which was his home and where his mother lives. When it came time to cut his leave orders following his second extension, the corporal did not designate his leave location, so the first sergeant assumed it was Baltimore and prepared the orders accordingly.

When it came time for his leave, Corporal Eason left his CAP, which was stationed in a hamlet near Ap Nam O and in the FLC area of tactical responsibility. Instead of going to the air base at Da Nang to catch his plane home, however, the corporal spent the next thirty days with his Vietnamese girlfriend at her home in Ap Nam O.

After the thirty days were over, Corporal Eason reported back to First Combined Action Group headquarters, where he met First Lieutenant Ziegler, who was on his way to the mailroom. Words were exchanged.

When Corporal Eason failed to show for his appointed departure on his leave date, this information was sent to his unit, and he was noted to be absent without leave. Although sources alerted the Combined Action Group headquarters that he was in Ap Nam O with his girlfriend during his thirty-day leave, he was still technically absent without leave because he failed to follow his leave orders to go to Baltimore. Naturally, the Marine Corps has to know where its people are and expects even leave orders to be obeyed. At the same time, Eason's commanding officer was tolerant. Corporal Eason had a good combat record and a good disciplinary record. Although he intended to call in Corporal Eason to give him a strong lecture and a warning about the importance of following orders, the colonel did not intend for Eason to face a court-martial. He even saw some humor in the situation, which led to Lieutenant Ziegler's comments to Corporal Eason when he showed up at headquarters: "Corporal Eason, the colonel wants to see you. You didn't follow your leave orders, and he is going to chew you out. He wants to see you first thing!" The lieutenant then added, "Don't get uptight; the colonel thinks this is kind of funny."

The evidence then shows that when Lieutenant Ziegler went back to the mailroom, Corporal Eason went to a gun rack, picked up his M-16, and shoved a fresh magazine of tracer rounds in it. After he chambered a round he walked into the mailroom. The three men working the mail turned as Eason entered, and the corporal, with the muzzle of his rifle, motioned the two enlisted men to move out of the way. He then pointed his rifle at Lieutenant Ziegler and said, "Funny, huh?" and emptied the clip into him.

When the deafening noise of the automatic-rifle fire stopped in the mailroom, the corporal popped the empty magazine from his rifle and was preparing to insert a new one when the two enlisted men recovered from their shock and jumped him. In a rage they threw him to the ground as more Marines came running into the mailroom. Eason was beaten into bloody submission.

Lieutenant Ziegler was killed instantly. He was a former enlisted man and a fine officer, who had been promoted from the ranks. He left a wife and young children.

Corporal Eason was handcuffed and put under the close supervision of the two chasers, who took him by plane from Chu Lai to Da Nang, where he was then transferred to a jeep for the ride to the III Marine Amphibious Force brig. On the way Eason was placed in the backseat next to one chaser while the other drove. As the jeep went around a curve in the road, Eason suddenly reached over to the man next to him and jerked his .45 pistol from its holster. He was in the process of chambering a round when the driver quickly drew his own pistol, turned, and shoved the barrel under the corporal's jaw. He told Eason to drop the .45, or he would pull the trigger. Eason dropped the pistol, and the fight went out of him. When asked later what he had intended to do if he had escaped, he said that he intended to defect to the VC.

Corporal Eason's background is relevant. He grew up in a tough neighborhood in Baltimore, where he was raised by his single mother. While other boys in the ghetto joined gangs and ran into trouble with the law, Eason was an acolyte in the Catholic Church. His mother emphasized the importance of working hard in school and in keeping an unblemished record. After graduation from high school, Eason volunteered for the Marine Corps.

Postscript: On his appointment as defense counsel, Jack Provine immediately filed a motion for a psychiatric evaluation of his client. This evaluation had to be conducted at the naval hospital in Yokosuka, Japan, and took some time to arrange. By the time the evaluation was completed, I had rotated home. In the meantime, the Marine Corps sent Corporal Eason back to Quantico, Virginia, for trial, where he was represented both by civilian counsel and by a Marine lawyer, but his request that Jack Provine be brought to Quantico to defend him was denied.

Because of my earlier involvement with the case, I was appointed to prosecute the case at Quantico. The main dispute was the mental competency of Corporal Eason at the time he shot Lieutenant Ziegler. The defense's theory was that Corporal Eason had snapped from being in Vietnam too long and that he did not have the ability to form the intent necessary in order to commit murder. The entire psychiatric staff from Yokosuka, Japan, was brought back to testify, and multiple experts were likewise called to testify for the defense. During the week of trial, the defense offered into evidence a diary that Corporal Eason kept while in Vietnam, including the thirty days he was in Ap Nam O with his girlfriend. They were attempting to show that nowhere during that time period did Corporal Eason ever express any animosity toward Lieutenant Ziegler, so there was no motive for the shooting. I took a noon recess to thumb through the diary and then had no objection to its introduction into evidence. When the time came for cross-examination, I used the entries made by Corporal Eason during the thirty days he was with his girlfriend to have him confirm, day by day, how relaxed and normal he was during this time. I argued to the court that insanity is not turned off and on like a water faucet. If a person is mentally disturbed to the point of insanity, his actions would have reflected this disturbance long before the actual act of the shooting. Eason's own diary rebutted his claim of mental disturbance and resulted in his conviction.

Corporal Eason was found guilty of murder, was reduced in rank, and was given confinement for fifty years. I felt a keen responsibility, throughout the preparation and trial, of the need to speak for Lieutenant Ziegler and his family. This was not the end of the story, however.

On appeal, the United States Court of Military Appeals reversed the verdict of the first trial because the Marine Corps had not made Captain Provine available when Corporal Eason had requested him. A subsequent trial was handled by other Navy and Marine lawyers. This time Private Eason was found guilty of a lesser offense than murder and, with credit being given for his time already served, was released and discharged from the service. Both Earl Ziegler and Charlie Eason were casualties of the war.

22 / Keeping the Pressure On

21 March 1969

We have survived two intelligence reports of impending doom at FLC and are awaiting the future cheerfully. Twice we received word that two NVA regiments were ready to start the last phase of their offensive, but nothing has happened. On the fifteenth, we conducted a cordon and search of Xom Long, and after the initial confusion of surrounding a village in the dark with a group of 120 men, we closed the cordon and sat down to await the dawn. At daylight, the National Police arrived and summoned the people into a collection center for interrogation while we probed for bunkers. The processing of the people was our best bet for obtaining information. We had launched the operation on the tip of Fifth Counterintelligence that VC were moving into the village in small groups to gather taxes and propagandize the people. There was a new blacklist, and we hoped to catch some of the local Mafia unawares. By 11:00 AM we had wrapped the whole thing up. The Chieu Hoi who had been seated at the interrogation table with the interpreters kicked them each time we brought up a Vietnamese who was a VC. We netted three hard-core VC from the operation, one of whom had been fighting as a guerilla since 1965. They were taken into a nearby building by the Vietnamese police for "questioning" about bunkers and caches in the area. There was no noise from the shack, but occasionally a policeman would walk out quickly, grab a length of rope, test it, and stalk back in. Or with their queer sense of humor, some of the young-looking police would come

Jack Provine and I at the cordon and search of Xom Long, March 1969.

out laughing and point inside, making motions like cutting a throat or hanging someone. Fifteen minutes later, the prisoners reappeared, all with swollen eyes and faces, but otherwise unharmed. The next day, one of them led
us to two bunkers, one of which had medical supplies and hand grenades.
We destroyed the bunkers.

Fifth Counterintelligence has compiled a progress report on our company that makes me proud of their efforts. Since 1 December 1968, our patrols have detained more than two hundred suspects for interrogation. Out
of these two hundred, the names of approximately fifty were on blacklists of
known and confirmed VC. We have killed or captured another ten to fifteen in action, thus accounting for more than sixty VC out of our area. Of
the sixty, about thirty-five were infrastructure members who propagandized,
collected rice and taxes, and attempted assassinations. The rest were fighters
or supply carriers. There are other ramifications that we rarely hear of. From
the two VC who were captured from the bunker when Gatz was wounded,
information was obtained on the location of the sapper company's base camp
in the mountains, and Phantom jets were called in for an air strike. The
next day, after the strike, Marine patrols swept the area and found six enemy
bodies.

Last week, one of our patrols was probing Hill 12 behind Ap Trung Son

John Reilly talking to children after the cordon and search of Xom Long.

and uncovered the body of a woman. She was buried in a remote area, without a tombstone or a casket. Fifth Counterintelligence believes she was a guerilla whom the Americans had killed and the VC buried. How many others have we accounted for that we do not know about?

The other night I went on a typical patrol, a long walk out over slippery, muddy, tottering rice paddy dikes while we sweated and waded in leech-filled streams. When we finally set in at our ambush site, the flies and mosquitoes tried to make a meal of us, and then the wind came up and froze our shirts to our skins. We lay in the mud, waiting for dawn or the enemy. Tired, cold, and hungry, I found my mind was mostly one thousand miles away and years off as I thought of the happy days of my boyhood. We thought we spotted a figure creeping off in the paddies and fired three M-79 rounds at it, but a sweep of the area brought negative results. Finally, the sky slowly began to brighten, roosters crowed, birds broke into song, and another day had come. The sun resembled a deep-red fireball as it rose through the mists. The rusty wheel of life began to turn again.

Da Nang has been hit by rockets and mortars with increasing regularity this past week, and we have again received reports that the long-awaited ground attacks are about to begin. We have another such report tonight, but I am dubious. I am more concerned with small bands of infiltrators, especially with local elections scheduled in the villages two days from now and the Communists' desire to stop them.

26 March 1969

I have two general courts today and am sitting here waiting to start. One of the accused, Private Alonso DiCastro, ought to be interesting. His first reaction on being told he was going to be tried was to ask, "Who are the court members? Who do I pay off?" The cases are just two more of the legion of marijuana cases. They are so routine and commonplace that I can scarcely be excited about them.

4 April 1969

It has been another hectic period, but a proud one. On 29 March I received word that Fifth Counterintelligence had an updated blacklist on the VC in

Xom Long. With the new list, they hoped to pick up a maximum of fifteen people and to get an AK-47, a carbine, hand grenades, and two pistols. Jack Provine is now one of my platoon commanders; I went with his platoon over to the Army compound until 4:00 AM, when we departed for the cordon and search. This platoon has outstanding morale, and Jack will make them a good leader. Sergeant House, Third Squad leader, is a tall North Carolinian and keeps everyone loose. We were sitting in the sand after the troops were briefed and drinking some coffee when Sergeant House came over and asked me whether I would like some sugar. I said all right, and he dropped a twenty-pound sack of sugar in my lap. Everyone broke up, and I told "Private" House that I appreciated his looking after me. Then there is Sergeant Parker, First Squad leader, who is a professional in every sense of the word. Staff Sergeant Hoffman is the platoon sergeant and has done a fine job, doubling often as platoon commander. Staff Sergeant Hoffman is a bit over thirty but looks more like thirty-seven, yet his enthusiasm is matched only by his stubbornness. Then, too, there is kindly looking Sergeant Harrington. Sergeant Harrington is on the heavy side, wears spectacles on his nose, and scarcely looks like he belongs in a young man's war; nevertheless, he is the platoon guide ("Pappy") and carries more equipment through the paddies than most eighteen-year-olds.

The cordon went perfectly, or as well as night operations can go when more than one hundred men are involved in three groups requiring coordination in the dark. We clamped a circle about the village by 5:00 AM and at first light swept the villagers from their houses to the collection points. To make short of it, we captured the local area VC youth leader (an eighteen-year-old boy) who that afternoon led us to an empty bunker that we blew up. We captured the VC security chief (a young eighteen- or nineteen-year-old girl) as she was trying to slip out of the village. We also captured five other VC on the blacklist.

Two nights later, I was on another night patrol with Third Platoon in the northern part of our area of responsibility, but we came home empty-handed. The following night, however, the Army helicopter compound across the road from us was hit by mortars, and at the same time one of our squads from its ambush position sighted the enemy. They opened fire and fought a vicious little firefight against the enemy's security screen for about fifteen minutes. Corporal Ed Johnson was the squad leader. He is the platoon demolition expert, and he directed the attack on the VC. At one point in the action, they were so close that Lance Corporal Paul Brandel saw a Vietnamese blasted to the ground, and he ran out under fire to pull his body back, along with his AK-47. At first light, the sweep of the area did not reveal any more bodies, but the next day, two more were found in shallow graves. They were all NVA.

This has also been a satisfying time for legal work. I tried two cases as the prosecutor, back-to-back, the other day after returning from my last patrol. The first involved Radames Gomez, a young Marine from Maintenance Battalion, who was caught with marijuana on three separate occasions, the marijuana totaling one hundred twenty-five sticks. We fought the case all the way. I won the search-and-seizure issue, and then it was tossed into the court's lap. The accused was under the influence numerous times, and marijuana was found on his person, in his boots, under his bed, and in his living area. The court found him guilty. Later, in the hearings prior to sentencing, the accused was put on the stand, and he revealed that he had been in the Da Nang area only three days before committing his first offense. He termed the command here "petty." This was the magic word that won the hearts of the court. He was awarded total forfeitures, a bad-conduct discharge, reduction to private, and confinement at hard labor for four years.

The following day Private First Class Edmund Stout went on trial for having 362 cigarettes of marijuana. He had also threatened two different Marines on different occasions by telling them that if they told anyone about his activities in the area they would never leave Vietnam alive. To show that he meant business, he and one of his bully boys beat another Marine senseless, breaking two of his teeth and closing his eyes with cuts that required a five-day no-duty chit for him.

Stout was well named—a blond-haired, short, husky, and muscular twenty-one-year-old who had a swagger and sneer on his face when he first came into court but that gradually faded from his pudgy face. By the end of the trial he had the hunted look of a trapped rodent, with his eyes darting back and forth anxiously. "Fast Eddie," the boy's nickname, traded government goods from his contacts in Supply Battalion to the Army and Seabees for beer; dealt with the Koreans and Vietnamese for contraband; and ran a wholesale business in marijuana. He was a "big man" and had everyone around him under his thumb. He finally overreached, however, when he beat one man too many and scared another into going to the authorities. Fast Eddie's career ended with a bad-conduct discharge, total forfeitures, reduction to private, and eight years' confinement at hard labor.

It was interesting to watch Stout's friends who lived in his hut and who perjured themselves for him. They swore that Corporal Collins, who had been beaten, had actually attacked the accused instead of vice versa. They claimed they had never seen the accused smoke or possess pot and so forth. They all congregated about him during recesses and loudly laughed and joked how it would be over soon and how generally it was all "no sweat." They began to sweat when their good buddy was found guilty. They all looked stunned when the court awarded him the eight years' confinement at hard labor. Now investigations are being run on these maggots, and some can expect their own trials.

The true character of the trial was Captain Wyman N. Jackson, the law officer. He is an imposing, granite-jawed, white-haired naval captain who presided over the proceedings and constantly scorched the young counsel. He left the imprint of his size twelve double E boots on my buttocks time and time again. He gave us hell, but he did it to teach us how to become lawyers. He chewed and growled and almost swallowed us. We were harassed, intimidated, and corrected, but I realized there was often a glint of humor in his eyes as he berated us in out-of-court hearings. I learned a tremendous amount about trials from him and appreciated his compliment on my preparedness after the courts were over.

5 April 1969

The night patrol that came in this morning had investigated an explosion and flash they observed on a rice paddy dike. A twelve-year-old peasant girl had stopped to rest and sat down on a VC booby trap, which blew her apart. Farther down the dike, another booby trap was discovered and blown in place. It is rice-gathering time now, and the VC are active. We are, too. A cordon and search of Ap Xuan Thieu is scheduled for 7 April.

23 / Easter and Operations in the Spring

6 April 1969

Easter Day. A cold wind and shredded clouds have been whipping out of the northern mountains all day. I attended church and again heard the good news of the Resurrection. Like most holidays here, however, it was rather anti-climactic. To top off Easter, at 2:00 PM the chief of staff hit on the brilliant idea of putting out gas canisters in the battalion area and gassing the base to see whether everyone had their gas masks handy. I jumped in a jeep and left the area prior to this memorable occasion. As I left, the gas was rolling in a billowing cloud over the camp. It takes a sick mind to do that on Easter.

8 April 1969

I was up this morning at 2:30 AM to run a cordon and search of Ap Xuan Thieu. What is surprising is that the operation even took place. Our battalion security officer was supposed to notify our battalion commanding officer of the operation and then coordinate with Fifth Counterintelligence and the Vietnamese. He did not do any of this; he somehow thought the operation was scheduled a day later. As a result, we were literally contacting Fifth Counterintelligence and the Vietnamese as we left our base. The actual operation itself was the smoothest we have run. Maybe the last-minute coordination kept our plans a secret. For our efforts, we picked up the two female

New friends.

VC agents we wanted. One had just returned from a base camp in the hills where she received extensive training. Both women have been guerillas since 1966, and if they talk they should have important information.

I left the operation at 7:30 AM and returned to base before driving out to Second Combined Action Group headquarters for the trial of a Navy corpsman who accidentally shot an M-79 and in doing so killed a Vietnamese. Jack Provine defended the boy and obtained an acquittal. Jack does a consistently fine job and is a natural trial lawyer. It is always fun to try a case with him and is also a humbling experience when he pins my ears back. A pompous, self-important major was the president of the court. He called Jack and me in to chew us out for not notifying him personally of the date and time of the court, for our lack of common courtesy to him, and for the short notice he had received. He proceeded to tell us how the court would be run. "Yes, sir, yes, sahib!" Jack pulled me aside and said, "Who's going to challenge this jerk off the court, you or me? If you won't, then I'm going to blow him out of the water!"

Sure enough, as soon as the court opened, the major began to criticize both of us while trying to impress everyone with his knowledge. Then it came time for challenges. Jack challenged the major off the panel so quickly that it was as if he were run out of town on a rail.

We returned to base that night and found an invitation to the house of a Vietnamese woman lawyer in downtown Da Nang. It was her birthday as well as that of Chuck O'Connor, a Navy lawyer downtown. Both were giving a party at her house, a thick-walled French colonial type in a very run-down neighborhood that had seen better days. It was a strange but enjoyable evening. She invited ten young Vietnamese girls, from seventeen to nineteen years old, who were very pretty and reminded me of little sisters. They obviously wanted a chance to try out their English, and I felt overly polite, like I was at a foreign students' mixer in college. It was also a little difficult to say much about the conduct of the war by the South Vietnamese and remain polite. I wore a fixed grin on my face and helped myself to the free drinks. We talked and dined by candlelight while a talented Navy enlisted man played the guitar and hauntingly sang. One of the songs was "Hey Jude" by the Beatles. The blend of cultures and the power of youth made for a cheerful and memorable time. The girls sang traditional Vietnamese songs and popular American ones for us and, in their shy ways, were very relaxing company. Lurking in the background were some Vietnamese officials and politicians who obviously were trying to sound out American feelings and intentions on Vietnam. Without a total commitment by the South Vietnamese to resist Communism, I am afraid that the shadows are rapidly closing in on all the actors in this brief interlude.

23 April 1969

On the thirteenth, my company participated in another multibattalion-sized cordon and search operation of the Ap Nam O area with the same lousy results as before. Technically, everything went smoothly except that in the dark hours of early morning, First Platoon, which I was with, became strung out so that its squads became separated. First Platoon had the job of connecting up with a platoon from Delta Company of the First Battalion, Twenty-sixth Marines in the vicinity of the Vietnamese PF camp. For security reasons, the Vietnamese in the PF camp were not told in advance of the operation, and we meant to stay well away from them until daybreak. As it was, Lieutenant Joe Dillard's point man, who was guiding the platoon, lost his way and led us right next to the perimeter wire of the PF camp, and because the PF had not been informed of the operation, if they spotted us moving around,

(Left to right) Lieutenants A. D. Skroch, Gene Schwartzlow, and Joe Dillard, all of whom were platoon commanders.

we were likely to be mistaken for VC and shot. Two-thirds of the platoon sneaked past successfully, but the last squad became separated from the rest of the platoon and froze in place outside the PF camp's wire. I went back and found them and went man to man, quietly letting them know that I was not happy that they let themselves become separated from the rest of their platoon. I expected at any moment to be fired on from the PF compound. I had the squad move away from the compound in the direction of a tree line and houses when a startled Vietnamese voice called out from the PF compound. A flare went up, and a shot cracked out. I buried my nose in the rice paddy, but my young hide was saved by Joe Dillard firing a green identification flare from his position on the other side of the village.

Thereafter, all went according to plan except for one minor problem. The second lieutenant of the platoon from Delta Company became lost or was delayed, so his men were late moving into place. I was helping Lieutenant Dillard locate his troops in the cordon when I heard a voice excitedly shout our call sign from the dark: "Mortgage, Mortgage, is that you, Mortgage?" I went out and led the men into their position because I had the advantage of knowing the local terrain.

This cordon had been planned by the South Vietnamese Army, and they requested our assistance in carrying it out. Nevertheless, they did not want to inform their countrymen in the PF compound because they did not trust them. As usual, the South Vietnamese Army troops started off early in the morning with gusto but ran out of steam by late morning. The people in the village were swept into the collection centers for interrogation, but our results were meager. We picked up one woman VC supply cell leader.

Although the results were meager, I was generally pleased with the outstanding job the men did in performing their mission. For some reason, everything seemed to click once we survived our brush with the PF troops. Later that day, I met the captain who was the commanding officer of Delta Company when he drove out in his jeep. He appeared rested, and he joked that he had come up with an excuse to avoid going on such a routine project. He seemed like a likeable person, and I tried to be on good terms with him. He asked me whether I could find him a lightweight nylon rain suit to take with him when their battalion went afloat again, and I told him I would do what I could for him.

That night, I relaxed at our bar while the rest of my friends in the legal office sang songs around an old appropriated piano and rolled dice for the drinks. I felt content.

24 April 1969

The day before yesterday, I returned with Jack Provine and his Third Platoon after a two-day sweep of Thuy Tu Island, called "the claw" because of its shape, an island to the north of us and out of our area of responsibility. First Battalion, Twenty-sixth Marines cleared us for the operation. Thuy Tu Island is actually a large peninsula jutting out into the Song Cu De River, and it is laced with small inlets. It is checkered with hedge groves that are choked with bamboo thickets and banana trees and is situated immediately across the river from the main infiltration routes leading out of the mountains to the north. We planned to probe the island for tunnels and caches by day and set up ambushes on the river by night.

We traveled by amtracs from C Company's position, which was located on the beach near the mouth of Da Nang Bay, and then churned our way upstream to come in from the rear of the peninsula via an inlet. I rode in the second of the three amtracs made available to us. As we left the main part of

Ap Nam O Village and the Ap Nam O Bridge as seen from a helicopter. The Song Cu De River flows into Da Nang Bay, with Thuy Tu Island ("the claw") in the background.

the river and were grinding and churning through the muck of the inlet toward our landing place, a metallic-like explosion went off under my amtrac. An antipersonnel mine blew out a fuel line, leaving the big, crawling machine disabled. There were no casualties, and we transferred to the other two machines and continued on into the island. This did not auger well for the expedition because we had word that a platoon from C Company had tried to penetrate the island the week before and had suffered four casualties from booby traps in fewer than ten minutes. We landed without further incident and proceeded to push through the jungle, leaving one squad with machine guns in a blocking position while the other two were to sweep and probe through the island. Then our planning fell apart.

The heat was brutal and exhausted everyone as we worked through the thick vegetation and hedge groves. By midafternoon, our water was already mostly gone, and our resupply for the night had been cancelled due to lack of available choppers. The river was salty, so, using water purification tablets, we drank from pools of stagnant water formed in the bottoms of shell-hole craters. The island was much larger than anticipated and took more time to sweep than was originally estimated. Thuy Tu turned out to be a huge, natural, and fortified defensive position. Although we blew up more than twenty-five bunkers and spider holes, there was not time to deal with them all, and literally hundreds remained. There was also the constant fear of booby traps. Every hedge grove had L-shaped trenches at its base that were connected to spider holes or bunkers, and they were each mutually support-ing from the adjacent hedge grove. If the VC were pushed out of one system, they had exits where they could fall back into an adjoining hedge grove and continue the fight. A battalion would have a hell of a fight clearing this nest out without extensive use of supporting arms. A platoon could be isolated and wiped out in a matter of minutes. Fortunately, we did not encounter any booby traps. This makes me think that the island has been cleared for entry from across the river by large VC or NVA units who can use it as a staging area prior to the start of the next phase of their offensive on the Da Nang perimeter.

Jack and I left the rest of the troops in the midafternoon and crawled over the island to locate the best ambush sites for the night. As we returned to the squad that was in a blocking position, we found three Marines, includ-ing the squad leader, far out in the middle of the river, swimming for the other side. They were towing over demolitions to destroy a cave they had spotted on the other side of the river. This act on their part caused us big problems. Although they blew the cave entrance, they went out of our opera-tional area without authority and were spotted by D Company's watchtower on a nearby mountain and mistaken for VC. As a result, they were fired on by small arms from D Company, which also came very close to calling in an artillery mission on them. At this point, D Company's commander came on the battalion radio network and chewed us out until the wire sizzled and mentioned throwing us out of their area. In the extreme heat, the coolness of the river overcame good sense, and this meltdown almost got our Marines killed. Everyone concerned felt abashed by the incident, particularly after I chewed them out, which only made their tired outlook more depressed.

At sunset we moved from our assembly positions into our ambush sites, but it was another long night with no contact. Farther down the river, sev-eral boats containing VC were caught by D Company trying to cross and were sunk.

The next morning we swept the island and blew more tunnels. In the center of the island we found a brand new Chicom hand grenade lying in the middle of a path. Apparently it had been accidentally dropped by a VC moving through the area the previous night while we were in our ambush positions on the edge of the river.

We had more problems this morning when D Company's CO thought he spotted us out of our area again and went berserk over the radio; however, it was not us this time. By 1:00 PM we moved off to the nearest road, where trucks picked us up. We had secured some interesting intelligence despite the problems yesterday. The Delta Company CO then called over to FLC and asked when he could come over and pick up that rain suit that he had originally mentioned to me during the Ap Nam O operation. I told him that we were fresh out.

2 May 1969

Hurray, hurray, it's the lusty month of May! Last Sunday, April 27, the ammunition supply dump at Camp Monahan exploded. Apparently brush fires had been burning for two days in the area, and one flamed out of control on Sunday, which ignited white phosphorous explosives, which, in turn, set off the rest of the massive dump. Fireballs and tremendous shock waves churned out of that tortured piece of earth for more than twenty-four hours. Large installations around the area were flattened by flying shrapnel and had to be evacuated. The air base was partially closed, and many Vietnamese homes were destroyed. There were sixty-four civilians and Marines hurt, with two killed. Investigations could reveal negligence in the running of the dump that might affect the careers of many men. The brig had to be evacuated, and the prisoners were brought to FLC for temporary shelter, where they promptly rioted.

19 May 1969

Ho Chi Minh's birthday. I have not written in over two weeks. I think day runs into day so quickly now that I am becoming lazy. For the last several weeks we have been receiving intelligence reports on pending enemy moves from the tenth of May through the twentieth in order to present Uncle Ho a birthday gift. On the fourteenth, I went with Sergeant Parker's squad and set in an ambush on Pagoda Island near the river. We used a new miniscope instead of the starlight scope and found it to be lighter and easier to carry, but we did not see any VC activity. Then, the South Vietnamese Army captured a VC message stating that at 3:00 AM on the morning of the eighteenth, the NVA/VC were to launch their offensive. On the sixteenth one group of forty NVA and another of ten to twelve hit the CAP unit adjacent to FLC and to our west. They killed the CAP commander and a corpsman and wounded two Marines while losing ten people themselves.

On the night of the seventeenth/eighteenth, I went on patrol to cover the approaches to our north and west. The people were all fairly new and inexperienced, but they hustled to do a good job. We set up on an island, put out claymores, and positioned the machine gun, laws, and riflemen. I organized my magazines of ammo and hand grenades so that I would be ready if we ran into infiltrators. The night crawled by, and I thought a great deal of home. We saw nothing, however.

There has been a big turnover in the office personnel now. Lieutenant Colonel Haden, Major Moore, Pete Mastaglio, and Chuck Cherry have rotated home. There is obviously a distinct change. No longer are lawyers crawling over each other, hooting and laughing at mealtime, dragging tables together, and pinching the Vietnamese waitresses. The new office staff seems more intent on operating the legal office like the military!

Last night I was on duty as the battalion officer of the day when one of my company sergeants came into the COC to alert me about a problem. A platoon from Truck Company at Dong Ha was in camp, and a baseball game, accompanied by hot dogs and beer, was arranged with a supply unit. A combination of youth, heat, and beer led to disagreements about the umpire's calls and resulted in two opposite groups facing each other, each armed with whatever clubs or other weapons they could get hold of. The two opposing ringleaders were into name calling but no direct contact when I stepped between them. All I could think of was to keep everyone talking until things calmed down. My sergeant, who came with me, kept asking if I wanted him to get the names and serial numbers of all involved. I did not want that. I wanted things to remain low-key. The parties continued to talk and seemed reluctant to disperse. Because we were next to the Provisional Rifle Company ready tent, I played the old-warrior card. I told the agitated Marines that they were disturbing troops who had been out all day and needed rest. Gradually, the assembled group began to break up and drift away. This is when I saw one of the Marines from the ready platoon standing back with a hand grenade in his hand. He just wanted to help, but his idea of help could have gotten us all killed.

24 / Final Days

20 May 1969

Rotten night's sleep last night! The air base was hit six times, and Mournful Mary, the siren, sent me stumbling from my rack to the bunker, dragging my thumping heart along behind. Nothing hit FLC. I dislike being awakened to be a spectator at someone else's drubbing. Our time in the barrel is past due.

It's been a real bitch of a hot day today, and I sit gasping for air like a big salamander. I inspected Third Platoon this afternoon, and by the time I reached the last rank, one man had collapsed, and the rest were tottering. First Platoon is out in the field on a two-day operation now, and I know their brains must be frying.

30 May 1969

A short pause to pay my respects to a fine officer and a very good man. First Lieutenant John Abbott, I have just learned, was killed in action today when he was hit by a mortar round. I am surprised and upset—surprised mainly that a close friend should die and upset at what his sacrifice may have accomplished. Despite the courage and commitment of men like John Abbott, we have no plan for victory, and each death erodes public support.

John was one of the infantry watch officers in the FLC COC. He helped coordinate and provide support for units in the field. He planned on making

Lieutenants A. D. Skroch and John Abbott.

the Marine Corps a career but was restless because his job kept him inside a bunker. He put in for a transfer to Third Marine Division in order to lead an infantry platoon, and I know that it was not a decision he took lightly. He was concerned about his wife and new baby but would laugh and say, "Hell, she's a damn good-looking woman, and if anything happens to me, she can take care of herself!" He could have stayed at FLC, transferred out of the COC, and become one of my platoon commanders. That would have been the easy way. The last time I saw John, he was passing through FLC on his way to meet his wife on R&R in Hawaii. He was enthusiastic and proud of the men in his platoon.

I lost three men to a booby trap last week. One will be medivaced to the States. The company also ran another cordon and search of the Xom Long hamlet, netting us 650 pounds of rice (American-aid rice that was being smuggled to the North Vietnamese in the hills), two low-level supply cadre, and four teenage village guerillas. A dozen of these semi-illiterate peasants are not worth one John Abbott, but one of them can kill you.

Today, I enjoyed the opportunity to be with other lawyers from different units stationed in I Corps at a meeting of the I Corps Bar Association. It was a perfect afternoon spent at the Seabees' beach facing Da Nang Harbor. We had plenty of steaks, beer, sun, and touch football in the sand, all with the deep blue of the ocean and the surrounding mountains wrapped in rain clouds for a background. I treasure the friendships that I have developed with some outstanding individuals. Colonel John De Barr made his farewell speech as our law officer. He has worked like a mule, and the strain has shown the last several months. He was relaxed and very nostalgic as he bid us farewell. Also today Charles Babcock was given June 3 as his flight date home. My departure should be twenty days after him.

8 June 1969

I have been given five days of leave in Japan by our new colonel at the legal office, and I have thoroughly enjoyed each moment. Today is my last day in the land of the industrious, highly disciplined, organized, and polite Japanese. My tour is more than a year old now, and soon I will be home. The high point of the trip was to take the bullet train from Tokyo to Kyoto and tour the ancient temple city. Japan is one of the most interesting places I have ever seen. I have been stuffed in a little Japanese hotel in the north of Tokyo next to a scenic park. The bed is low to the floor and has hard pillows, and the thick quilt covering makes me feel like the center portion of a sandwich. Their house shoes (too small) in each room and a kimono are not meant for Westerners.

I have visited the countryside and the city by walking and by going on different tours. I took a one-night tour that included a geisha party, a sukiyaki dinner, kabuki theater, and a floor show. For the dinner and geisha party, we had to take off our shoes, and I was the only one with his toes out of one sock.

I have met more Australians here, and I find that our personalities always seem to click at first sight. Alwyn and Carmel Smith are from Lae, New Guinea, and were my company to Nikko. I met several beautiful American girls on the tour as well, including the 1969 Maid of Cotton and her escort. I wanted them to join me for dinner the night before I returned, but, alas, they had other plans.

As my tour has been winding down, I have been thinking of our world. I believe that time has run out for wars on a grand scale. We are too interdependent on one another for it to make any sense, and if history has taught any lessons in the past century, it seems to me that it has shown conclusively that no nation is fit to govern another. Only a serious miscalculation by the Communists, a change in the temper of the American people, or a historic accident should throw us into another world war.

Never again should we let a country like South Vietnam dictate our foreign policy. Because of our opposition to Communism and our support for more freedom in the world, we have been trapped into supporting a weak regime that lacks the support of its own people. To offset the corruption and inefficiency of the South Vietnamese government, we have "Americanized" the war. Where do we go from here?

14 June 1969

I returned from Japan and then on the ninth and on the tenth went to Dong Ha to try a staff sergeant who had been charged with negligent homicide for shooting a marijuana-smoking Marine who tried to run from him when ordered to stop. The court debated the verdict for three minutes and found him not guilty. Given the fine prior record of the sergeant and the equally poor record of the victim, I was not upset with the verdict. Tom Schwindt and I tried to grab a late flight out of Dong Ha back to Da Nang but could not. Because we had a big thirst and the dust was clogging our mouths, we managed to find ourselves in the nearby Third Tank's club. There we ran into Captain Dan McQueary and his freewheeling hospitality. Dan runs a tank company out of Con Thien, and they come back to be refitted, take showers, and receive new clothes about once a month. We all proceeded to become mentally deranged, swapped war yarns and lies, and had an enjoyable time. The tankers took us to their huts to spend the night and insisted on giving us their beds ("We wear the same uniform, don't we?"). In the morning Dan gave me a coffee transfusion and took me out to his tanks. He showed me how they operate, including their weak points and strong points, and generally impressed me with his good common sense.

19 June 1969

On the twelfth, in the early evening about 6:30 PM, I was just walking out of my hooch when I heard loud explosions and saw the dust rising out on the edge of our perimeter. I assumed it was some of our demolitions people at work until I heard a shrieking roar scream by overhead and explode behind me. The rest of the rounds found me huddling in a deep hole. The attack was short and sweet (no casualties) and seemed something of a parting shot, an anticlimax to my tour. I walked to chow and found that the rounds had the happy side effect of cleaning out the mess line and that I had the place to myself for a quiet meal.

On the fourteenth, Tom Schwindt, John Reilly, and I caught a truck convoy to An Hoa to see what the countryside looked like. Some railroad cars had been found sitting there for the past ten years, and the Marines were supposed to retrieve them for the Vietnamese and bring them back to Da Nang to be rebuilt and put into service. All the way down, air and artillery strikes pounded the hills to give us breathing room. We passed camp after camp carved into the tops of small hills, crisscrossed with trenches and barbed wire, and covered by the inevitable cloud of red dust. An Hoa itself was not much to brag about. Situated inland, it did have some fairly nice-looking civilian homes located on small hills, but it remained mainly a military camp. On the way back, I saw a Marine company involved in an off-road sweep. They were dispersed and taking mortar rounds, but I could not see where the fire was coming from.

On the fifteenth I turned over command of the Provisional Rifle Company to Bob Walker as I began to wrap up my tour in Vietnam. Bob is an excellent Marine. He is a first lieutenant now but in the Korean War was a corporal when he fought his way out of the Chosin Reservoir with the First Marine Division. He has vast knowledge and experience and has not hesitated to share them with me. He has been a great friend, and the company will be in good hands.

On the seventeenth I took Third Platoon out to participate in a company-sized cordon and search of Mieu Thach Son. Jack Provine had just returned from R&R and was in no shape to go, so I took his platoon. I learned one fine lesson. I do not like to be second in command, particularly in a situation where I have been used to calling the shots. Although Bob Walker is a good leader, and I will always consider him as one of the best officers I have met here, there is something personal about command that one has to lose before he can appreciate it. When in command, a man takes the risks but makes up his own mind and does what he thinks best under the circumstances. This is personally more satisfying than following someone else's orders. We set up

Change-of-command ceremony for the Provisional Rifle Company, 15 June 1969. First Lieutenant Bob Walker *(left)* takes command as I rotate home.

our ambushes early in the evening and about 2:00 AM broke to head for our position in the cordon and search. Our ambush site was behind paddy dikes and looking out into the open paddies. I had not been sitting in the mud long when I began to experience an intense itching all over my buttocks. Later, when we set in for the cordon, it seemed to grow worse. I nearly ran for the showers when we returned to base, but soap and water brought no relief. I was forced with clenched teeth to go by sick bay, where I was told I had been sitting in a patch of ticks. I empathize with dogs now.

Our cordon netted only one confirmed VC. The main person we were after, a young girl, escaped. The next night, however, the company repeated the operation, catching them all by surprise. They (I was back in camp, drugged on medicine to ease my itching) caught the girl, another VC, and two South Vietnamese deserters. I found out this morning that the siren had blown as a warning of incoming, but I was so tired and doped up that I slept right through it. This operation marked the end of an era of my life. I doubt that with less than a week left in-country that I will go back out. I think that I will miss these times. These have been days when I have felt most alive.

25 / Going Home

On 24 June 1969 it was finally my time to climb on a bus at the Da Nang airfield and be carried to the area where passenger jets were landing and taking off. When our plane's engines revved to a high pitch and the aircraft rolled down the runway and lifted off the ground, cheers exploded from the homeward-bound Marines. It was a dream to be going home and to be able to totally relax.

We landed early the next morning in San Diego. Although it was 5:30AM, we were greeted by kindly, silver-haired volunteers, who had coffee, juices, and donuts for us and wanted to thank us for our service in fighting Communism. While I appreciated their support, I was a little uncomfortable with the political tone of their greeting. I was tired and eager to go home, and I did not comprehend how much America had changed during the year I was gone.

I then flew on a commuter airline to Los Angeles, where I was to catch a plane to Dallas and then on to San Angelo. Walking up to the ticket counter, I saw a nineteen-year-old tanned blonde goddess handing out boarding passes. As I stared in wonder at her, she coolly looked me in the eye and asked me how many babies I had murdered while I was in Vietnam. I was speechless in the face of her open hostility.

In the airports, I found that people simply ignored me. That was fine by me. Of course, when I finally arrived home, I was overwhelmed by the reception I received from my parents, my little sister, and my friends. My older brother was now back in Vietnam as an advisor to the South Vietnamese Marines. The problem was that it was very difficult to explain to others what my life had been like over the past year. We were on different wavelengths. After a few weeks of leave, I was ready to report to Quantico, Virginia, where I was assigned to teach law at The Basic School.

On my way to Quantico, I stopped in Mississippi for a visit with my old friends Jim and Jody Brown. Jim was out of the Marine Corps by this time and commented, "Griff, you really don't know what war is until you have to bury a member of your family." His cousin who was a second lieutenant in the Army and an infantry officer had recently been killed, and it weighed heavily on Jim.

After I reported for duty at Quantico, I spent many weekends going to Washington, D.C., for entertainment. We were not allowed to wear our camouflaged utilities off base and were discouraged from wearing any uniform in Washington. I soon understood why. Frequent antiwar demonstrations took place on a weekly, if not a daily, basis. It was strange to go into our nation's capital after coming from Vietnam and to watch as thousands of people marched in mass demonstrations carrying North Vietnamese and Viet Cong flags. Although I was not in uniform, my short hair indicated that I was in the military. This generally gave some anonymous hero in the crowd an incentive to throw his drink on me.

Happily, I ran into Pete Mastaglio from FLC, who had been transferred to the base legal office at Quantico, and I made other new friends easily. I enjoyed teaching the new lieutenants, and I also participated in court-martials. Life was still full until I received a phone call around 6:00 PM on January 25, 1970, shortly before I was due to go out for the evening.

The call was from Lieutenant General Lewis Fields, the base commander at Quantico. The general and his family were our family friends after my brother, Bill, served as his aide at Camp Pendleton, California. He simply said: "Don, this is General Fields. I think you need to call home. Your mother needs to talk to you." I immediately began to apologize for the inconvenience. I assumed that my mother had called the general and asked him to locate me when she could not reach me. She did not understand the military. Mothers did not call generals to relay messages to their junior officer sons. At the same time, I was also struck by the kindness in General Fields's voice. When I finally rang through to my parents, my mother answered and told me the painful news that every parent prays to be spared. Bill had been killed in action. His wife, Sally, was at home in San Angelo, where she had just given birth to their second daughter. Before making arrangements to come home, I needed to go to Bill and Sally's apartment in Woodbridge, Virginia, to locate Bill's will.

It was a dark, lonely trip to Woodbridge. I was crying and thinking about what had to be done when I heard my brother's voice inside my head. It was calm and peaceful, and he said, "Well, Brother, it's up to you now." I know that I was distraught, but through the years I have not forgotten the message.

Time has passed and lessened the intensity of Bill's immediate loss. He left a fine wife and two beautiful daughters, who are now mothers themselves. I have learned the lesson that God does not give a person more than he can handle. I have also learned that along the way happy surprises occur. The greatest in my life has been to meet and marry Priscilla Chase, my anchor in the world, and through her I have been blessed with four wonderful children.

America is now involved in another conflict, this time in Iraq, which is a clash of religions and cultures with roots going back for centuries. Will, our oldest son, has served in Iraq as a Marine first lieutenant. Some things don't change. I have seen in him the same sense of purpose, pride in the men he served with, and the anxiety over the unknown that I felt years ago. I feel fortunate to have spent some key years of my impressionable youth being part of a team much bigger than myself and risking all for what I believed to be the cause of freedom. I would do it all again tomorrow.

Glossary of Military Terms and Acronyms

ammo | Ammunition.

amtrac | Amphibious tractor; a military vehicle that moves on tracks on land and in water.

article 32 investigation | Preliminary investigation conducted to determine whether there are enough facts to justify the filing of charges against an individual.

ARVN | Army of the Republic of Vietnam; South Vietnamese troops.

battalion | Military unit consisting of four or five companies.

BCD | Bad-conduct discharge.

C-4 explosive | Plastic explosive.

CAP | Combined action platoon; typically composed of one squad of U.S. Marines (thirteen men) and two squads of South Vietnamese Popular Forces (a home-guard type of troops). They lived in the villages to provide protection from the Communist forces and to deprive the Viet Cong guerillas access to recruits, taxes, and information.

C (Charlie) Company | My training company at The Basic School, Quantico, Virginia.

Charlie | See "Viet Cong."

chaser	Armed guard responsible for transporting prisoners.
Chicom	Slang for hand grenades of the enemy. Word stemmed from the words "Chinese Communists."
Chieu Hoi	Viet Cong defector.
CO	Commanding officer.
COC	Combat Operations Center.
Company	Unit made up of three or four platoons and normally containing between 100 and 180 men.
CP	Command post.
D (Delta) Company	Rifle company in Twenty-sixth Marine Regiment that operated in a tactical area of responsibility adjacent to Force Logistics Command.
DMZ	Demilitarized zone. Technically this referred to the no-man's-land separating North and South Vietnam. In practice, the entire area that bordered that no-man's-land was referred to as the DMZ.
F-4U	Jet fighter.
fire team	Smallest tactical unit in the Marine Corps; consisted of four men.
FLC	Force Logistics Command, the supply unit that provided the supplies to all Marine units in I Corps.
FLSG	Force Logistics Support Group; a separate administrative command within Force Logistics Command. Included were FLSG Alpha and FLSG Bravo.
fragging	Act of criminal behavior where typically the perpetrator would roll a fragmentation hand grenade under an officer's sleeping quarters in order to kill or injure him.
general court martial	A type of trial proceeding reserved for felony offenses where punishment of certain offenses may involve the death penalty and where confinement exceeds one year in prison. The court consists of a minimum of five officers and senior enlisted personnel.
grunt	Slang term for infantryman.

gunship	Armed helicopter.
H&S Co.	Headquarters and Service Company; the command, intelligence, communications, and logistics center for a Marine unit.
hooch	Living quarters at FLC that typically had a wooden floor elevated off the sand by short piers. The sides were surrounded by mesh wire, and the roofs were made of corrugated steel. They had front and back entrances and usually slept six to eight men.
Huey	UH-1 helicopter.
incoming	Hostile fire.
in-country	Service within the Republic of South Vietnam.
K-bar knife	Standard Marine Corps fighting knife.
law	Light antitank weapon.
M-16	The standard rifle used by U.S. forces in Vietnam.
M-60 machine gun	The standard lightweight, belt-fed machine gun of all U.S. military forces in Vietnam.
M-79	Shoulder-fired, single-shot grenade launcher.
medivac	Medical evacuation.
MOS	Military Occupational Specialization.
MP	Military police.
NCB	Naval Construction Battalion.
NCO	Noncommissioned officer; corporals and various grades of sergeant.
NVA	North Vietnamese Army. The term used both in the singular (referring to single soldier) and in the plural.
office hours	Disciplinary procedure under the Uniform Code of Military Justice for limited punishment from an individual's commanding officer.
on line	Reference to Marines sweeping an area or otherwise engaged while spread out and moving side by side.
PF	Popular Forces

platoon	Unit made up of three squads and typically commanded by a second lieutenant; usually consisted of thirty-five to fifty men.
PLC	Platoon Leaders Class
Provisional Rifle Company	Ad hoc infantry company formed with personnel from various component organizations who served in a dual capacity—part-time operating as infantrymen and part-time performing their regular military specialties.
R&R	Rest and relaxation.
recon	Reconnaissance.
road master	Motor transport officer in charge of scheduling drivers and vehicles.
S-4	Logistics office.
sapper	NVA or VC soldier trained to overrun and destroy positions using explosives.
Seabees	U.S. Navy's construction battalion.
short timer	Person nearing the completion of his thirteen-month tour in Vietnam.
slit trenches	Narrow trenches used as protection from enemy mortar and rocket attacks.
special court martial	Type of trial proceeding used for the trial of less-serious offenses involving sentences of confinement of 365 days or less. The court-martial panel is made up of a minimum of three officers.
spider hole	Concealed enemy foxhole.
TBS	The Basic School, located at Quantico, Virginia, is where every beginning Marine Officer went through five months of intensive training to learn the basic information and skills required to be a Marine Officer.
Uniform Code of Military Justice	The codified system of criminal law, evidence, and procedure followed in the military.

VC   Viet Cong, also referred to as "Victor Charlie" or "Charlie." These were the Communist South Vietnamese who carried on guerrilla warfare in the cities and countryside of South Vietnam.

Index

Page numbers in italics refer to photographs.